The Healing Secrets of the Ages

OTHER BOOKS by the Author:

THE DYNAMIC LAWS OF PROSPERITY
THE DYNAMIC LAWS OF HEALING
THE PROSPERITY SECRETS OF THE AGES
THE DYNAMIC LAWS OF PRAYER
(formerly PRAY AND GROW RICH)
OPEN YOUR MIND TO PROSPERITY
OPEN YOUR MIND TO RECEIVE
THE SECRET OF UNLIMITED PROSPERITY
DARE TO PROSPER!
THE PROSPERING POWER OF LOVE
THE PROSPERING POWER OF PRAYER

―――――――――――――――――

"The Millionaires of the Bible" Series

THE MILLIONAIRES OF GENESIS,
Their Prosperity Secrets for You

THE MILLIONAIRE MOSES,
His Prosperity Secrets for You

THE MILLIONAIRE JOSHUA,
His Prosperity Secrets for You

THE MILLIONAIRE FROM NAZARETH,
His Prosperity Secrets for You

―――――――――――――――――

All the above books are available from DeVorss & Company

The Healing Secrets

OF THE AGES

Catherine Ponder

Published by
DeVORSS & COMPANY
P.O. Box 550, Marina del Rey, CA 90294

ISBN: 0-87516-550-8

LIBRARY OF CONGRESS
CATALOG CARD NUMBER: 67-26503

PRINTED IN THE UNITED STATES OF AMERICA

CONTENTS

rash. The healing power of color and music. A nurse heals another person through imaging. Healing power of a wheel of fortune. How to make a wheel of fortune. Picturing shortens the distance to your goals.

Where understanding is located. How intuitive understanding heals. Your feet are connected with the mind power of understanding. Affirmations to increase healing through understanding. The power of light to heal. How to use light for healing. You have the wisdom of Solomon. Healings that occurred through using intuitive understanding. The peaceful state of mind healed him. How to attain your good more quickly. How to develop the vast benefits of wisdom. Intuitive understanding comes alive in quietness. Cases of mental illnesses healed through intuitive understanding. Understanding has a solution for every problem.

The location of the will. Nothing wrong with will. Health problems caused by willfulness. Marital discord caused by willfulness. How to treat willfulness. Willfulness is mental murder. Willfulness brought confusion and mental illness. Choice of the right kind of will. God's will is for your good health. Dare to call on God's will for you. Another's will can cause disease for you. Your "must" powers for healing.

Location of the order center in the body. How your order center functions. The wonderful results of divine order. The effect of order on female problems. Overcome challenges with order. Turning failure into success. How to quicken this healing faculty of order. Demonstrate good health through divine order. Changes you can expect from divine order. The infinite blessings of divine order. An aggravated bladder condition healed. An Oxford graduate proved the joys of divine order. How divine order can bring much good to you. One of the highest forms of prayer.

Introduction . . .

YOUR DYNAMIC MIND POWERS!

Once, after hearing me lecture at the Civic Auditorium in Pasadena, California, a reader of mine waited in a long line to tell me his own amazing healing story.

A few months previously he had been confined to his bed with what had been diagnosed as an incurable lung disease. As I understand it, his lungs had expanded and become spongy, and there was little hope of his recovery.

A neighbor brought this sick man a copy of my book, *The Prosperity Secrets of the Ages,* in which there are related a number of stories that emphasize man's incredible healing power. As he began to read the book and apply its healing ideas, this very sick man recovered! A few months later he was standing in that long line relating his story: "I am supposed to be dead, but through changing my thinking, I have been healed."

Later I checked with a doctor about this type of illness and the doctor only shook his head, "If a patient came to me in that condition, I would try to make him as comfortable as possible and would advise those caring for him to do the same, but that's about all I could do, since no cure has been found for that type of disease." When I related this man's experience, the doctor replied, "It must have been a spiritual healing. There is no other explanation for it."

Such is the story of mankind's incredible healing power.

Several decades ago, when I wrote this book, it already cost 50 million dollars to build a medical school and another five million a year to run it. With daily escalating costs, one cannot properly estimate what it would cost today.

How much money and emotional stress and physical pain we could save if people knew of the incredible healing power located right within them which they can deliberately activate and benefit from, and which is of vast assistance to the family physician as he treats them.

Unfortunately, most folks take better care of their cars than of their health or of their states of mind, which so strongly influence their health! This places an undue burden upon the family doctor in trying to heal them.

YOUR 12 HEALING POWERS

In one of my other books, *The Dynamic Laws of Healing*, you will find related many stories of healings that have occurred in the lives of people in all walks of life who learned of the power that their thoughts and feelings had upon their health.

That book covers many vital points on healing which there is not room to repeat here. In this present companion book, I assume you have a general understanding of the material previously discussed and that you are now ready to consider other phases of mental and spiritual healing.

In these pages I wish to share with you incredible healing secrets known and invoked by the great minds down through the ages. They are teachings that have been well-guarded and passed on from century to century to just a select few. These teachings have remained a well-guarded secret even until this day.

These secret teachings have to do with the *12 mind powers* located within the vital nerve centers in your body, which greatly affect your health, either constructively or destructively, depending upon how you are using these mind powers.

In modern times we have heard much about the power of man's glands and how the state of man's health depends upon the state of his glands. This is true, but for more than physical reasons. The state of a man's health is strongly affected by the state of his glands because the nerve-gland areas in the body are also centers of vital mind powers. These vital mind powers located right within the glands have been unconsciously functioning all the time, often to the detriment of man's health because of his ignorance of their presence within him. How man uses these mind powers located in the gland-nerve areas vitally affects his health constructively or destructively. *These are the well-guarded healing secrets of the ages!*

I first learned of these secret teachings when I took up the study of practical Christianity and heard these mind powers described as "the 12 powers of man." Their mystical significance is linked with Jesus and His 12 disciples in the New Testament, and with the 12 tribes of Israel in the Old Testament.

Occult philosophy has long recognized that there are

seven mind powers located in seven vital nerve centers in the body. The 12 powers of man simply embrace and expand these seven natural powers into 12 divinely mental powers, making them easier to understand and use. The number 12 has always been regarded as a sacred number of completion in the development of man's higher powers.

THESE POWERS HAVE HEALED COUNTLESS PEOPLE

A Missouri realtor, Charles Fillmore, and his schoolteacher wife, Myrtle, learned something of these amazing powers within them at a time when they both had supposedly incurable diseases. (Their healings are described in Chapter 1.) As the Fillmores began developing these mind powers located right within their bodies, not only did they overcome "death sentences" and live a number of active decades thereafter, but in the process they founded one of the most far-reaching healing movements of this century known simply as "Unity," because its teachings unite the great truths of all ages.

There are those who say that it is only as a person becomes spiritually and mentally enlightened that he unconsciously begins developing these 12 deeper powers of the mind. I have not found this to be true. On the contrary, during the years I have been actively engaged in the ministry and have been searching out the laws of mental and spiritual healing, I have observed that in almost every instance of ill health that came to my attention, some of these 12 mind powers were invariably being misused by the sufferer! Often he had little or no spiritual enlightenment — that was why he had come to me for help.

Obviously, these 12 mind powers were functioning to some degree within his mind and body, though perhaps on a weak subconscious level. Nevertheless, their misuse was affecting his health adversely. It seemed apparent that if a person had some knowledge of these 12 mind powers, he could begin deliberately developing them constructively from a conscious level, rather than allowing them to continue haphazardly functioning on a subconscious level only. Accelerated healing power within his mind and body would then be the natural result. After making this discovery, I determined to learn all I could about these secret teachings and share it with all mankind. This book is the result, and it brings good news to you!

There is still hope for you to live a healthy life as you learn about these indwelling mind powers, how misuse of them affects your health adversely, and how right use of them can aid you in becoming healthy again.

For instance, you will discover that a person who is "down in his back" was first down in his thinking, usually because of financial problems, as he misused his mind power of Strength located at the small of the back. You will discover that critical people are inclined to misuse their mind power of Judgment located at the pit of the stomach. Indigestion, ulcers, even possibly cancer of the stomach are the natural result. You will discover that hurts in the love nature, expressed as disappointment, bitterness, resentment, possessiveness, and unforgiveness, cause trouble in the lungs, breast, chest and heart area, which is the center of the mind power of Love in the body. Heart trouble, asthma, tuberculosis, or cancer of the breast can then result.

You will discover that problems in the organs of elimination in the body result because certain negative emotions have not been eliminated from the mind power of Elimination located in the intestines, kidneys and other organs of elimination in the abdomen. You will discover that *disease always has a mental correspondent with one of the 12 mind powers located in the body.* This knowledge removes the mystery from disease and leads you up the enlightened road to permanent healing.

I am happy to report that in the intervening decades, since this book was first written, I have received numerous healing reports by readers who consistently worked with the ideas contained in the forthcoming pages.

Go quickly now to Chapter 1 and begin to learn *the secrets* in far greater detail. Then, as you get busy applying them through knowledge gained in the succeeding chapters, you will probably have your own healing story to relate! With Solomon, you may even find yourself joyously declaring: "Counsel is mine, and sound knowledge. I am understanding; I have might." (Proverbs 8:14)

CATHERINE PONDER

The healing secrets of the ages

NOW REVEALED

— 1 —

One cartoon pictures a frustrated businessman leaving a hospital room carrying his bags, trailed by his wife and nurse. On the way out he gripes, "Those darn miracle drugs. I just got in bed and here I am out already!"

What that man does not realize is that unless he discovers the mental cause of his ailment deep within his own feelings, he will probably return to the hospital for more of those "darn miracle drugs." Whereas, if he understood something of the healing mind powers located right within his body and how to activate them, his bouts with ill health could be avoided.

The healing secrets of the ages reveal that you have 12 dynamic mind powers, which are located in 12 dominant nerve centers right within your body. It is a surprise to most people to find that these 12 mind powers are not all located in the brain in the region of the head as we might assume. Instead they are located throughout the body. Brain thinking cells are found throughout your physical being. This intelligence is waiting to be recognized and released for its healing mission. Thus, your whole body is really mental and thinks!

ANCIENT MAN USED THESE POWERS

This is not a new discovery. *References to the 12 mind powers in man are found in the oldest documents dealing with human beliefs and practices. The ancient Greeks, Persians, Egyptians, and Hindus felt that every part of the body had a secret meaning, and their priests placed statues of man's body in their temples in order to study its secret meaning.*

Ancient seers, long before the time of Christ, believed there were 12 "cosmic centers" in man, which if understood and controlled, could release tremendous power into his mind, body and affairs. The mystics of the Orient, both in symbol and secret formula, revealed to their students something of this teaching. The Jewish philosopher, Philo, and the Greek philosopher, Aristotle, hinted at these powers in man, as did the German physician, Paracelsus, when he spoke of "energy cores."

Edwin John Dingle, Founder of the Science of Metaphysics, relates in his book, *My Life in Tibet*,[1] how he was taught to release tremendous energy located in various parts of the body many years ago by his Tibetan master. Edgar Cayce, in his famous trance readings, referred to the mind powers located in the glands as an ancient teaching.[2] Also, the age-old science of astrology

1. Edwin John Dingle, *My Life in Tibet* (Los Angeles: Econolith Press, 1939).
2. Gina Cerminara, *The World Within* (New York: William Sloane Associates, 1957). See the chapter, "The Endocrine Glands."

has long taught that if there is balanced thought, there is always balanced glandular activity, and vice versa.

May Rowland, former Director of Silent Unity, through her famous *A Drill in the Silence*,[3] has shown thousands of people how to arouse these powers within them for increased health and peace of mind. Her own youthful vitality amid a full, demanding life was a valid testimony to the power one can release through deliberate development of these 12 mind powers.

Noted scientist and medical doctor, Alexis Carrel, explained how the body is enveloped with mind power, which can be directed and controlled:

"The mind is hidden within the living matter . . . completely neglected by physiologists and economists, almost unnoticed by physicians. Yet it is the most colossal power of this world."

Concerning how this indwelling mind power affects the body, Dr. Carrel wrote:

"Each state of consciousness probably has a corresponding organic expression. . . . Thought can generate organic lesions. . . ."

Concerning how we can direct and control thought and its effect on the body, he wrote:

"When our activities are set toward a precise end, our mental and organic functions become completely harmonious. . . . In order to keep his mental and organic balance, man must impose upon himself an inner rule."[4]

3. May Rowland, *A Drill in the Silence* (Unity Village, MO: Unity School of Christianity). Available in pamphlet and on cassette.
4. Alexis Carrel, *Man, The Unknown* (New York: Harper & Row, Publishers, Inc., 1935).

SCIENCE SUBSTANTIATES THE EFFECT
OF MIND ON BODY

The mysterious effect of man's mind upon his body appeared far more important to our ancestors than did his physical aches and pains. Metaphysical study attracted far greater men than did the study of medicine for many centuries. Ancient physicians attributed vast importance to man's temperament and idiosyncrasies in connection with his health. It has only been since the Renaissance of the sixteenth century that the *effects* of ill health have been so greatly emphasized, rather than their mental and emotional *causes*. Fortunately, in recent years, the pendulum has begun to swing the other way again.

Today, our scientists and doctors realize that man has within him great powers which he fails to use. Some medical doctors claim that 75 percent of us are using only 25 percent of our physical powers. We are not even half alive! The father of American psychology, William James, said many years ago that 90 percent of us are using only 10 percent of our mind power:

> "Compared with what we ought to be, we are only half awake. We are making use of only a small part of our mental and physical resources. Stating the thing broadly, the human individual thus far lives far within his limits. He *possesses powers of various sorts which he habitually fails to use.*"

In terms of energy, scientists tell us we are filled with a super-atomic power; that there is enough stored in the cells of the body to destroy a city, if released in a certain way. Most people are not aware of this power because it is a part of the deeper levels of the mind.

Modern psychologists go even further in their claims than did William James: they estimate that man *uses only 1/10 of 1 percent of his energies and powers. The rest of his forces are lost because they are expressed outward instead of inward.* Apparently it is an age-old problem because the ancients felt that all problems resulted from "under-nourishment"—mostly mental and spiritual—and that *all transmission of energy was from within.*

Medical scientists substantiate this. They state that *man is a self-renewing organism; that each of us has enough energy within him to run a universe, if he but knew how to release and control it!* Edison went so far as to state that his investigations had convinced him the human body is composed of trillions of atoms, each of which is a center of intelligence; and if man could gain control of this innate intelligence through his will, he could live forever!

Twenty centuries ago, the Great Physician, Jesus, tried to point out the source of man's unlimited indwelling powers when He said to the doubting Pharisees, "The Kingdom of God is within you." (Luke 17:20) And our modern psychologists are just now beginning to discover the wisdom of Paul's advice to the Romans: "Be ye transformed by the renewing of your mind." (Romans 12:2)

HOW THE HEALING OF TUBERCULOSIS CAME TO MYRTLE FILLMORE

Myrtle Fillmore, mother of three boys and wife of a Kansas City realtor, in the year 1886 learned that she had tuberculosis, which was then considered an incurable disease. She was given just six months to live.

On a warm spring night, her husband took her to attend a metaphysical lecture. Having had a traditional religious background, the Fillmores knew nothing of the power of thought to heal, but were desperately willing to consider any constructive technique that might restore health.

At the lecture the speaker said, "You are a child of God; therefore, you do not inherit sickness." This was an electrifying idea to Mrs. Fillmore, who had been led to believe that she had probably inherited her supposedly incurable tuberculosis—a further reason why nothing could be done for her.

In the pamphlet, *How I Found Health,* Mrs. Fillmore relates how she turned her energies within instead of without, and how she imposed upon her thinking that "inner rule" of which Dr. Carrel wrote, and thereby realized healing:

> "I have made what seems to me a discovery. I was fearfully sick; I had all the ills of mind and body that I could bear. Medicine and doctors had ceased to give me relief, and I was in despair when I found practical Christianity. I took it up and I was healed. I did most of the healing myself, because I wanted the understanding for future use. This is how I made what I call my discovery:
>
> "I was thinking about life. Life is everywhere—in worm and in man. 'Then why does not the life in the worm make a body like man's?' I asked. Then I thought, 'The worm has not as much sense as a man.' Ah! *Intelligence as well as life is needed to make a body.* Here is the key to my discovery. *Life has to be guided by intelligence in making all forms. The same law works in my body.*
>
> *"Life is simply a form of energy, and has to be guided and directed in man's body by his intelligence. How do we communicate with intelligence? By thinking and talking, of course. Then it flashed upon me that I might talk*

*to the life in every part of my body and have it do just
what I wanted. I began to teach my body and got
marvelous results.*

"I told the life in my liver that I was not torpid or in-
ert, but full of vigor and energy. I told the life in my
stomach that it was not weak or inefficient, but
energetic, strong, and intelligent. I told the life in my
abdomen that it was no longer infested with ignorant
thoughts of disease . . . but that it was all athrill with
the sweet, pure, wholesome energy of God. I told my
limbs that they were active and strong.

*"I went to all the life centers in my body and spoke
words of Truth to them—words of strength and power.*
I asked their forgiveness for the foolish, ignorant course
that I had pursued in the past when I had condemned
them and called them weak, inefficient, and diseased.
I did not become discouraged at their being slow to wake
up, but kept right on, both silently and aloud, declaring the words of Truth, until the organs responded."[5]

Immediately her health improved. Within two years,
Myrtle Fillmore was completely well again, and she lived
another 40, happy, active years.

HOW THE HEALING OF TUBERCULAR ABSCESSES
CAME TO CHARLES FILLMORE

Meanwhile, her husband slowly accepted the possibility of healing: "Although I was a chronic invalid and
seldom free from pain, the doctrine did not at first appeal to me," he later wrote. Still, because he was a practical man, when saw his own wife's healing take place,
and that of others who came to her later for help, he

5. Myrtle Fillmore, *How I Found Health* pamphlet, (Unity
Village, MO: Unity School of Christianity).

could not ignore the fact that great power was being released, and he finally became interested.

Of his own gradual healing, he writes in his book, *Atom Smashing Power of Mind:*

"I can testify to my own healing of tuberculosis of the hip. When a boy of ten I was taken with what was at first diagnosed as rheumatism, but developed into a very serious case of hip disease. I was in bed over a year, and from that time on I was an invalid in constant pain for twenty-five years, or until I began the application of the divine law.

"Two very large tubercular abscesses developed at the head of the hip bone, which the doctors said would finally drain away my life. But I managed to get about on crutches, with a four-inch cork-and-steel extension on the right leg. The hip bone was out of the socket and stiff. The leg shriveled and ceased to grow. The whole right side became involved; my right ear was deaf and my right eye weak. From hip to knee the flesh was a glassy adhesion with but little sensation.

"When I began applying the spiritual treatment there was for a long time slight response in the leg, but I felt better, and I found that I began to hear with the right ear. Then gradually I noticed that I had more feeling in the leg. Then as the years went by the ossified joint began to get limber, and the shrunken flesh filled out until the right leg was almost equal to the other. Then I discarded the cork-and-steel extension and wore an ordinary shoe with a double heel about an inch in height. Now the leg is almost as large as the other, the muscles are restored, and although the hip bone is not yet in the socket, I am certain that it soon will be and that I shall be made perfectly whole.

"I am giving minute details of my healing because it would be considered a medical impossibility and a miracle from a religious standpoint. However, *I have watched the restoration year after year as I applied the power of*

thought, and I know it is under divine law. So I am satis-
fied that here is proof of a law that the mind builds the
body and can restore it." [6]

Charles Fillmore was healed as he experimented with, called forth, and finally wrote about the fantastic mind powers located right within the body, which he later described as "the 12 powers of man." He personally proved that a person can develop and release these dynamic mind powers and overcome almost unbelievable health problems. Later at the age of 84 he wrote, "I find I am releasing electronic forces sealed up in the nerves of the body. My physical organism is being transformed cell by cell." Mr. Fillmore lived another active, happy decade after this.

SCIENTIFIC PROOF OF THOUGHT'S POWER ON BODY

Does it sound fantastic to you that man has such unlimited powers for physical renewal within him, which he can deliberately release, as did the Fillmores?

This is not a new idea. A Yale University professor undertook to demonstrate the power that thought has on the body in a most scientific way at the turn of the century. He had a young man suspended in his laboratory on a perfectly balanced disk. He told the man, who was a mathematician, to think of some difficult problem in mathematics and to try to solve it mentally.

As the man began to think hard, the nicely balanced disk tipped on the side where the man's head was, the

6. Charles Fillmore, *Atom-Smashing Power of Mind* (Unity Village, MO: Unity School of Christianity).

blood flowed to the brain in increased amounts and that tipped the scale. He told the man to think of running, for the young fellow had been a football player and was interested in track events. And as the man began to think of making a hundred-yard dash or of running down the field with the ball under his arm, the disk tipped on the side where his feet and legs were. The blood was now flowing more freely into these organs.

By asking the man to repeat the multiplication table of nines, the displacement was greater than when he was repeating the table of fives, which is an easier table. The professor found that *the center of gravity in the man's body was shifted as much as four inches by merely changing his thought, without the moving of a muscle.* This professor literally proved that thoughts are things, and their power for good or ill can be accurately weighed and measured.

Here, then, is a power to be deliberately used! If the blood can be made to flow more freely here and there by a change of thought; if all the processes of digestion, assimilation, circulation and elimination can be influenced for good or ill by mental conditions; if all those functions, which are in constant communication with the nervous system, can be aided or hindered in their operation by the thoughts we think, then you can see why the healing secrets of the ages are so powerful. Indeed, the most vital functions we have—digestion, assimilation, circulation, and elimination—though unconscious in their action, are nevertheless constantly and profoundly influenced by the power of our conscious thoughts. This means you are not at the mercy of ill health. You can turn the tables on it through deliberately improving and then directing your improved thoughts!

WHERE AND WHAT THESE POWERS ARE

The healing secrets of the ages reveal that you have within you the following 12 mind powers, located right within the following vital nerve and gland centers in the body, as shown in Figure 1-1.[7]

1. The mind power of FAITH is located in the center brain at the pineal gland.
2. The mind power of STRENGTH is located between the adrenal glands and the loins at the small of the back.
3. The mind power of JUDGMENT is located at the pit of the stomach in the solar plexus near the pancreas gland.
4. The mind power of LOVE is located in the heart-chest area, back of the heart near the thymus gland.
5. The mind faculty of POWER is located at the root of the tongue in the throat near the thyroid gland.
6. The mind power of IMAGINATION is located between the eyes, near the pituitary gland.
7. The mind power of UNDERSTANDING is located in the forehead in the front brain, just above the eyes.
8. The mind power of WILL is located in the forehead in the center of the front brain.

---

7. Though I am indebted to Charles Fillmore's sketch as given in his book, *The Twelve Powers of Man,* published by Unity, thorough research into both ancient teachings and modern physiology made it necessary to rearrange the location of certain mind powers, from those shown in his original sketch, in order for them to correctly correspond to their gland locations.

Figure 1–1.

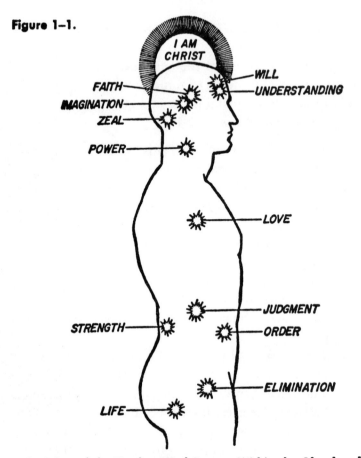

Location of the Twelve Mind Powers Within the Gland and Nerve Centers of the Body.

9. The mind power of ORDER is located at a large nerve center just behind the naval in the abdominal region, known in ancient times as the "lyden gland."

10. The mind power of ZEAL is located at the base of the brain in the back of the neck at the medulla.

11. The mind power of ELIMINATION is located in the organs of elimination in the lower back.

12. The mind power of LIFE is located in the generative organs.

Please note: Along with these 12 mind powers, there is also the I AM or Christ Mind which is located in a ganglionic center at the apex of the brain in the crown of the head. It releases a super-intelligence into all 12 mind powers when activated. Please note in Figure 1-1.

WHERE DISEASE IS LOCATED

Now that you know where these 12 mind powers are located, it is easy to see how misuse of them could cause definite physical ailments in various areas of the body, as well as affecting the entire body; whereas deliberate, constructive use of them could increase one's health and vitality in the different areas, as well as improve it throughout the body.

Even though these dynamic mind powers have been used sporadically by mankind down through the ages, it need no longer be a secret teaching considered fit only for the "advanced." These powers should be known and used by all humanity in this enlightened age. *It is time the whole world knew that disease is not so much in the body, as in the mind which envelopes the body; that disease is not so much in the nerves and glands, as in the mind powers located in those nerves and glands. You do not live in your body so much as you live in your thoughts and feelings which envelop your body.* This is where disease or lack of ease first occurs!

Actually, health does not come and go. *Health is eternally present!* It is our awareness of it that comes and goes, according to our moods and deep feelings which are constantly affecting the body. Doctors generally agree that the object of using their remedies is to quicken the natural functions of the body. *But medicine does not appeal to the intelligent principle that directs the natural functions of the body; hence, it fails to give permanent healing which can only come when that intelligent principle is released.* Nevertheless, medicine can be a welcomed relief from discomfort while man is learning to use his mind powers correctly.

HOW TO RELEASE THE INTELLIGENT
HEALING POWER

There is a divine current within you that carries healing power. As Mr. and Mrs. Fillmore and many others before and since them have proved, *your energy flows where your attention is directed. This is how you release the intelligent principle in the various parts of the body.* As you deliberately direct your attention and release the flow of energy, this calls into action the intelligent principle located in that area of the body and also stimulates energy throughout. Improved health is the natural result.

Again, this is not a new idea, but a proven ancient healing method. *Both the ancient Egyptians and Brahmans knew that by centering their complete attention they stimulated centers of consciousness in the body and healing resulted. They knew and proved that the powers of the conscious mind over the body are well-nigh immeasurable!*

Do not become tense about the exact location in the body of the various healing mind powers that are shown in Figure 1-1. Do not try to meticulously match up your aches and pains with these mind powers. Instead, while obtaining medical, chiropractic, or psychiatric treatment to relieve the immediate effects of certain health problems, *go a step further* and begin searching out their mental and emotional causes. The general location of your illness in the body will usually be an indication of the mind powers which have been misused.

Just as ancient philosophers believed that man goes throught 12 stages in his enlightenment, I suggest that you read this entire book through, learning of your 12 mind powers and how they affect your health. This knowledge helps you to metaphysically treat the *total man* rather than a specific disease. Thereafter, you can go to the mind powers that interest you most and begin developing them in connection with overcoming the health problems with which they are connected.

HOW THESE MIND POWERS WORK

These 12 mind powers deal with forces that function below and above the field of conscious thought. As you begin developing them, they may start working in ways you had not expected! Often they will first work in the subconscious phases of the mind to cleanse, purify, and free your emotions and body of thoughts, feelings, memories, old grudges, hates, and fears that stand in the way of your healing. *Indeed, the purification of the mind is one of the first steps necessary to permanent healing.* (Study Chapters 2, 3, and 4 in my book *The Dynamic Laws of Healing*[8] regarding this method.)

---

8. Catherine Ponder, *The Dynamic Laws of Healing* (Marina del Rey, CA: DeVorss & Co., 1966).

These mind powers may begin working in the super-conscious levels of your mind first, providing you with flashes of inspiration and guidance to be followed; showing you things to do that may seem totally unrelated to your healing. Yet, later you will see how these subconscious and superconscious phases of your mind had to be activated first before the conscious levels of your being could respond with a complete healing.

Thus, do not grow impatient and do not expect anything dramatic to happen suddenly. *In the laws of physics, you know that force exerted at one point acts simultaneously at every other point in substance. So it is with disease and with healing: it is never confined to just a single organ, but affects the whole body.* As you do your part, deliberately arousing your mind powers constructively, you can rest assured that the subconscious phases of the mind, which control the automatic functions of your body, will respond in their own time and way.

Just as a healthy body functions normally in silence, so you need not hear, feel, or even be aware of when the healing process sets in, though you may under certain circumstances. Sometimes it is only later that you quietly realize normality has been restored. *Peace of mind precedes bodily healing. When you get a sense of peace, that is an indication that healing is taking place.* From that point on, give thanks that you are being *healed!*

The word "doctor" literally means "teacher." The purpose of this book is not to replace your family physician, but to teach you how to constructively begin using the mind powers located in the various parts of your body, and to help you get at the mental and emotional *cause* of ill health in those areas. To that degree this book "doctors" as it teaches. Meanwhile, you should certainly continue getting medical help in relieving the accumulated physical *effects* of ill health if you want to.

A SECOND HEALING SECRET

In case you hesitate to develop these 12 mind powers, let me assure you that you have already been using, or misusing, them and you have been reaping a constructive, or destructive, result accordingly. Now, you can begin to use them wisely, confidently, and definitely for your increased and continued good health.

This leads us to a second all-powerful and little-known healing secret of the ages:

We have just spoken of the conscious, subconscious, and superconscious activities of the mind, which work through your 12 mind powers. These three activity levels of the mind are also located right within the body. When you know *where* these three mind activities are located, you will better understand whether it is your conscious or subconscious thinking that is causing various diseases. Also you will realize that releasing the energy from your superconscious mind activity into the other two can help alleviate the metaphysical causes of ill health. *Knowledge of this takes all mystery out of disease* and helps you to begin activating health within immediately!

The following paragraphs contain a detailed description of the three activity levels that are within you, as illustrated in Figure 1-2.

THE SEAT OF HEALING OF THE CONSCIOUS MIND

First: The seat of your conscious mind—which reasons, analyzes, ponders, consciously thinks—is located in the front forehead and extends into all the five senses. What you consciously think and deliberately say affects all your mind powers located from the forehead all the way down into the throat area.

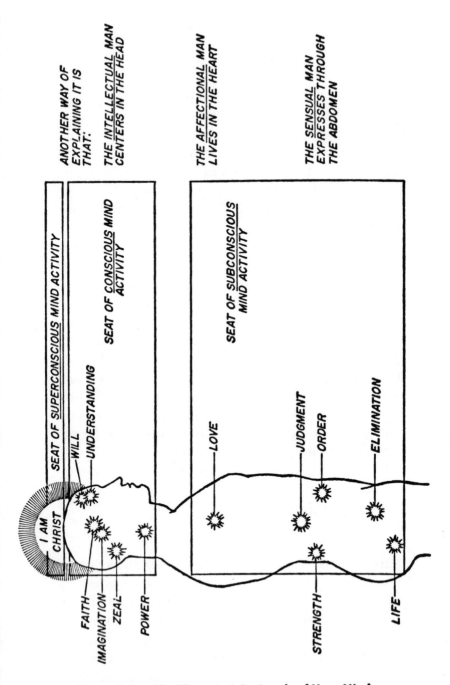

Figure 1–2. The Three Activity Levels of Your Mind.

1. The mind power of WILL located in the forehead in the center of the front brain.

2. The mind power of UNDERSTANDING located in the forehead in the front brain.

3. The FAITH mind power located in the center brain.

4. The mind power of IMAGINATION located between the eyes.

5. The mind power of ZEAL located at the base of the brain in the back of the neck.

6. The mind faculty of POWER located at the root of the tongue in the throat.

Misuse of any of these mind powers brings an almost immediate health reaction in that part of the body. For instance, a housewife quarreled with her husband and spoke strong, critical words to him. By misusing her power center located in the throat, within two hours she developed a sore throat and cold which took her two weeks to recover from!

The strong negative thoughts and words of others, expressed with feeling, can also cause one discomfort in the above areas of the body that are so strongly affected by the conscious mind—unless a person learns how to protect himself from such negativity.[9]

Knowledge of the fact that these mind powers are located in the area of the conscious mind indicates to you that health problems in the forehead, brain, ears, eyes, nose, or throat area are often caused by your most recent

---

9. See chapter on "The 'No' Power of Healing" in the *Dynamic Laws of Healing,* and chapter on "Protection" in *Pray and Grow Rich,* both books by Catherine Ponder.

conscious thoughts or by the strong, negative thoughts and words of others directed toward you. It also indicates that your present, deliberate, constructive thoughts can begin relieving health problems in these areas of the body.

Special Note: Though the conscious, subconscious, and superconscious activities of the mind function throughout the body and are definitely connected with certain portions of the brain according to medical science, we are instead pointing out here the *seat* of these three mind powers' *metaphysical* activities in the various parts of the body.

THE SEAT OF HEALING OF THE SUBCONSCIOUS MIND

Second: The seat of your subconscious mind activity in the body is located in the heart and abdominal region, which is the seat of your strong emotions and deep, even secret, feelings. What you strongly feel and are convinced about becomes a subconscious thought pattern affecting your mind powers located in this abdominal region.

1. The mind power of STRENGTH located in the loins at the small of the back.

2. The mind power of LOVE located back of the heart.

3. The mind power of JUDGMENT located at the pit of the stomach.

4. The mind power of ORDER located at the navel.

5. The mind power of ELIMINATION located in the organs of elimination in the lower back.

6. The mind power of LIFE located in the generative organs.

When you have physical ailments in the heart and abdominal region, it is often the result of unconscious emotions and feelings you no longer consciously remember: old hurts, prejudices, resentments, bitter emotions and memories of that past that are stored in that subconscious area of the body and cause havoc there.

For instance, people who have heart trouble, female disorders, kidney trouble, stomach trouble, and various elimination problems are usually carrying deep subconscious resentments toward people and experiences of the past which must be cleared out before permanent health can be restored in the abdominal region of the body. As you begin developing your mind powers, especially the six located in this area of the body, they will go to work for you to help you cleanse these negative emotions from the abdominal region of the body. Also, the strong thoughts and deep, perhaps secret, emotions of others directed toward you—of which you may or may not be aware, can affect your health in these areas of the body. As already suggested, use of the "no" power of the mind, and prayers of protection can help, in such cases.

THE SEAT OF HEALING OF THE
SUPERCONSCIOUS MIND

Third: The superconscious activity of the mind functions from the crown of the head. This mind activity is described as the Christ Mind, the I AM, or the center of Divine Intelligence and Wisdom since it has direct access to universal life and wisdom. Your sudden inspirations, intuitive leadings, flashes of perception, hunches, telepathic or other extrasensory perception powers function from this area. Also, dynamic energy is released from this area to flow to all the 12 mind powers and physical functions of the body.

The superconscious activity of the mind awakens and activates the most potent form of energy in the mind and body of man! Apparent miracles often occur when this Divine Intelligence is activated. It seems to release deeper mental and spiritual levels of the mind that can actually reverse the natural laws of the body, if necessary, so that the incurable is then cured.

You activate the superconscious level of the mind through spiritual study, through prayer, or through using affirmations which awaken this superconscious phase of the mind. The Spanish mystic of the sixteenth century, St. Teresa of Avila, described in her celebrated book, *Interior Castle*,[10] how spiritual powers were aroused in the upper part of her head as a result of prayer.

The people of the Old Testament affirmed the names "Jehovah" and "I AM" and the people of the New Testament affirmed the names "Jesus Christ" and "Christ Jesus" for this purpose. The first and second century Christians also wrought miracles after affirming over and over the Lord's Prayer, which released the Christ consciousness.

For 18 years a housewife had had an ear fungus which had eaten one ear drum completely away and had made a large hole in the other one. The germs lay dormant with a great deal of infection gathered close to the middle ear. When she sneezed or got water in this ear, it

---

10. Allison Peers, *Interior Castle* (New York: Doubleday & Co., 1961).

caused boils which would swell the ear canals, causing them to completely close up. This was also very painful.

She had spent a great deal of money on medical treatment. When her doctors made laboratory tests, they informed her there was no known drug or antibiotic that would destroy this germ. They were most concerned for her health since this infection was close to the brain and the middle ear.

After learning of the dynamic power that is activated through the superconscious phase of the mind, she released it during a painful attack by affirming over and over the words, *"Jesus Christ, Jesus Christ, Jesus Christ."* Within six hours the swelling and pain had disappeared and there was no more evidence of infection. Although this healing occurred several years ago, this housewife has had no more trouble with her ears.[11]

HOW THE THREE PHASES OF MIND
CONNECT FOR HEALING

You can also begin to develop the superconscious phase of the mind for healing by decreeing "DIVINE IN-TELLIGENCE." Apparently this was Myrtle Fillmore's secret in healing herself of an incurable disease: "Intelligence, as well as life, is needed to make a body . . . Life has to be guided by intelligence . . . Life is simply a form of energy, and has to be guided and directed in man's body by his intelligence. How do we

11. For developing the superconscious phase of the mind for healing, see chapters, "The Miracle Law of Healing" and "The Occult Law of Healing" in *The Dynamic Laws of Healing*; also see the chapter on "The Prayer for Miracles" in *Pray and Grow Rich*; and the chapter on the Lord's Prayer in *The Millionaire from Nazareth*.

communicate with intelligence? By thinking and talking, of course."

You can begin now to release the dynamic energy from the superconscious phase of your mind by relaxing daily, breathing deeply and affirming, "I AM DIVINE INTELLIGENCE. I AM. I AM. I AM. I AM LETTING DIVINE INTELLIGENCE EXPRESS PERFECTLY THROUGH ME NOW. I AM. I AM. I AM." Sweep your attention from the crown of your head, to the tip of your toes, as you declare this statement over and over. You can go even further by releasing this miracle power into your life and affairs as you daily affirm, "I AM SHOWN EXACTLY WHAT TO DO AT ALL TIMES AND IN ALL CONDITIONS. I AM ABLE TO DO EVERYTHING PERFECTLY NOW."

Affirming "Divine Intelligence" awakens the power of the superconscious in the crown of the head, and then unites it with the intelligence of the conscious mind in the forehead. The combined intelligence of both conscious and superconscious phases of the mind are then released into the subconscious activity of the mind located in the abdominal region of the body. Increased circulation and vitality are the natural result.

Through using this mental drill *daily*, you will find that you are soon feeling better, more alive, energetic, peaceful, and confident, and that a higher intelligence does seem to be at work in your mind, body and affairs, showing you how to live every phase of your life victoriously.

A THIRD HEALING SECRET—RIGHT AND LEFT SIDE BODY RELATIONSHIPS

There is yet one last healing secret of the ages that may also give you a clue to health problems. The ancients considered the right side of the body to be masculine, and the left side of the body to be feminine. In ancient times men fought with their right arm and defended with their left arm, in which they carried a protective shield.

The healing symbolism is this: If you resent someone of the masculine sex, you may have health problems over and over on the right side of your body, until you forgive and release that resentment.

The right-masculine side of the body symbolizes wisdom. If you have been misusing your wisdom, you may get a destructive result on the right side of the body over and over until you begin using your wisdom properly. (The foregoing affirmations on intelligence are helpful for this purpose.)

Also, the right arm is the giving arm and indicates that repeated health problems on the right side of the body show a need to give in some way. You have been withholding something on the physical, financial, mental, emotional or spiritual plane that you should be giving.[12]

Repeated health problems in the left-feminine side of the body indicate resentment toward someone of the feminine sex: a mother, mother-in-law, wife, daughter, sister, or some neighbor, friend, or business associate of the past or present.

Since the feminine gender also symbolizes love, if you have been misusing your mind power of love or letting your love be misused by others, perhaps in some secret or illicit way, it can cause health problems on the left side of the body.

Also the left side of the body symbolizes the ability to

---

12. See the chapters, "Your Giving Can Heal You" and "The Healing Law of Release" in *The Dynamic Laws of Healing*.

receive and then use wisely that which is received. If you have refused to receive certain good extended to you, or if you feel your good has passed you by and you have been cheated out of receiving it, you can begin to clear up health problems on the left side of the body that reflect those attitudes by opening your mind to the idea of receiving: "I AM RECEIVING NOW. I AM RECEIVING AND WISELY USING ALL THE GOOD GOD HAS FOR ME, AND GOD HAS UNLIMITED GOOD FOR ME NOW!"[13]

If you have accumulated a vast knowledge of Truth through intensive spiritual study, but have not used it to work out your life problems or to aid others, its stagnation can be found in health problems which have settled on the left side. Truth demands expression. You must use the Truth you know!

A housewife related how she could trace her own health problems to this great "right-left" healing secret of the ages:

> "My father was a very strong-willed person and always critical. He criticized me severely and was often upset over trifles. As a result of my secret resentment toward him I was constantly hurting myself as a child — always on the right side. I almost cut off my right finger when I was a child, and though the finger healed, the lymph nodes under my right arm became so sensitive that even until this day they will bother me, if I become upset. I also suffered very serious burns at various times on my right knee, the right side of my abdomen, and on my right foot. My appendix, located on the right side, had to be removed after a chronic infection.
>
> "My right hand was severely cut on two different occasions, once when my brother came to live with me; this

---

13. See chapter on Divine Restoration in the book, *Open Your Mind to Prosperity* (Marina del Rey, CA, DeVorss & Co., 1971).

was at a time when I did not feel I could afford to help him.

"Regarding health problems on the left-feminine side, once as a child my mother became very angry with me after she had been ill for several months. For many days she refused to speak to me. During that period a window glass fell on my left foot, almost severing my big toe. It was only after mother and I became friends again that it healed."

For the healing of recurring health problems on the right or left side affirm, "THE FORGIVING POWER OF DIVINE LOVE NOW FREES ME FROM ALL RESENTMENT OF THE PAST OR PRESENT. I NOW GO FREE TO BE HEALTHY AND HAPPY."

Do not try to absorb the three healing secrets of the ages given in this chapter all at once. Instead, just begin to acquaint yourself with these age-old healing truths. Later, as you become thoroughly familiar with them, you will be able to quickly analyze (from a metaphysical standpoint) the mental and emotional causes of distress in various parts of the body. Disease will no longer be a mystery to you, nor will the mental and spiritual methods of healing it!

SPECIAL NOTE: The book referred to herein as *Pray and Grow Rich* has been retitled, in a revised edition, *The Dynamic Laws of Prayer.*

Your healing power of

FAITH

— 2 —

The Archbishop of Canterbury once said, "It is a great mistake to suppose that God is only concerned with religion."

This same truth also applies to faith. The general belief that faith is something that has to do only with one's religious experiences is incorrect. *Faith is a mind power, and you are using it all the time.* It constantly affects your health, wealth and happiness—not just on Sundays, but seven days a week.

Anything you have faith in can become a result in your life. Mighty results may be attained through exercising even a small amount of faith.

William James in describing the power that faith has on your health said, "Faith is the habitual center of man's personal energies."

A SOURCE OF FAITH POWER

One of the healing secrets of the ages is that the first of man's 12 dynamic mind powers to develop is faith. The ancients believed that faith as a mind power was located in the pineal gland, just above the ears and adjacent to the eyes, at the center of the brain.

Little is known about this mysterious pineal gland, which has been called the "third eye," or "the eye of the gods." Until a few decades ago it was paid scant attention. Medical authorities believe that this gland regulates man's susceptivity to light, and that it may have definite effect upon the sex nature, as well as being related to brain growth. (See Figure 2-1.)

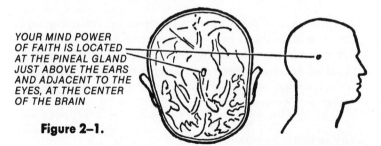

YOUR MIND POWER OF FAITH IS LOCATED AT THE PINEAL GLAND JUST ABOVE THE EARS AND ADJACENT TO THE EYES, AT THE CENTER OF THE BRAIN

Figure 2–1.

Location of the Pineal Gland (Mind Power of FAITH).

In small children there is an extremely sensitive area above the crown of the head where the skull does not completely close until the child is between seven and nine years of age. Prior to this, young children often display extreme sensitiveness and awareness, even having clairvoyant experiences that are generally believed to be connected with this "third eye" or pineal gland.

According to esoteric philosophy, one of the healing secrets of the ages is that this small cone-shaped gland at the center of man's brain has a very special function:

When it is stimulated, this gland presumably stands upright, permitting the essences of the brain to blend with the higher intelligence in man. This, in turn, releases tremendous power, energy, and wisdom not ordinarily tapped by man and produces amazing results quickly. In the process man has released the kind of faith that can remove mountains.

Regardless of its physical functions, the pineal gland or "third eye" is symbolic of that higher intelligence that is released into man's mind, body, and affairs when he activates his mind power of faith, located in the area of the pineal gland.

Charles Fillmore has described the incredible power one can release through this mind power of faith:

> "Just as the electric current precipitates certain metals in an acid solution, so faith stirs into action the electrons of man's brain; and acting concurrently with the spiritual ethers, these electrons hasten nature and produce quickly what ordinarily would require months of seed-time and harvest."[1]

Why is faith so powerful?

Because when you activate faith, you set into operation a mind energy that is thousands of times more powerful than electricity. Your mind power of faith then generates an energy that contacts the universal energy, and causes circumstances and events to be created that make your goal of faith possible! Indeed, activated faith releases a vibration that is endowed with a fantastic, attracting power. The drawing power of faith is not possessed by any other mind power.

---

1. *Atom-Smashing Power of Mind*, p. 125

HOW TO RELEASE FAITH

How does one release this electronic energy contained in the mind power of faith located at the pineal gland? Through speaking forth words of faith. *There is a healing power stored up in the body which is released through words of faith. When a word is spoken, a chemical change takes place in the body because the life current in man is subject to the spoken word. Thus, your words of faith have life-giving power!*

Faith is the only guarantee of immediate success in healing. He who becomes master of his faith can become master of his health because faith is a force that produces life-giving results! Jesus emphasized the power of releasing faith through the spoken word when He promised:

> "Have faith in God. Verily I say unto you, Whosoever shall *say* unto this mountain, Be thou taken up and cast into the sea; and shall not doubt in his heart, but shall believe that what he *saith* cometh to pass; he shall have it. Therefore I say unto you, All things whatsoever ye pray and ask for, believe that ye receive them, and ye shall have them." (Mark 11:22–24)

Faith moves ideas in the mind and causes them to express themselves. To have faith in God is to have a daring conviction of the goodness of God at work in your health and in your life.

When faith becomes active in you, you may get very restless and discontented with your world. This is an indication that faith is moving in your mind, trying to bring greater good into your life. This is the time to speak words of faith, such as these, "I HAVE FAITH THAT I AM NOW IN TUNE WITH THE UPWARD, PROGRESSIVE MOVEMENT OF LIFE. THE MARK OF SUCCESS IS UPON ME."

In *The Autobiography of Mark Twain,*[2] life along the Mississippi a hundred years ago is described. Doctors were scarce. When one could be found, he would care for the whole family for $25 a year. His fee included the medicine which he provided, usually castor oil, and it was prescribed by the dipperful! Since there were no dentists, the family doctor simplified matters by yanking out teeth with his tongs.

As for faith healing, Mark Twain relates:

"We had the 'faith doctor' too, in those early days — a woman. Her specialty was toothache . . . She would lay her hand on the patient's jaw and say, 'Believe!' and the cure was prompt."

When this faith-healer commanded her patient to "believe," she was actually doing a scientific thing. She stirred up the mind power of faith within the patient which released the electronic energies within the electrons of his brain. This hastened the action of nature and quickly produced healing results which might ordinarily have required much longer or might not have occurred at all.

An eminent scientist recently substantiated the fantastic power that faith has by stating that there is only one basic quality man must develop and exercise in order to tap the higher powers within him, so that his dreams can come true. That basic quality is simply the ability to *believe without a doubt*. The scientist explained that when man is able to do this, he enters a state of consciousness wherein *all* things are possible to him!

---

2. Charles Neider (ed.), *The Autobiography of Mark Twain* (New York: Harper & Row, Publishers, Inc., 1959).

FAITH HEALS ARTHRITIS FOR A BUSINESSMAN

A businessman was declared an incurable with what his doctor described as arthritis and neuritis. He was told there was no one on earth who could heal him.

Unable to work and to provide for his wife and seven children, this man was advised to take walks through the park and to make himself as comfortable as possible to help ward off the pain. This man intuitively felt that he could be healed if he could get his faith activated, so he visited his minister who prayed with him. Together they dwelled upon the Bible promise: "The prayer of faith shall save him that is sick, and the Lord shall raise him up." (James 5:15)

While following the doctor's orders and walking in the park one day, he spied a piece of paper lying on the ground near one of the benches. Faith is intuitive, and as this man intuitively picked up this scrap of paper, he found the key to his healing in the words of faith written on it. Fascinated by them, he memorized and repeated these words over and over, daily, even hourly:

"God is my help in every need,
God does my every hunger feed.
God walks beside me, guides my way,
Through every moment of the day.

"I now am wise, I now am true.
Patient, kind, and loving too.
All things I am, can do, and be,
Through Christ, the Truth that is in me.

"God is my health, I can't be sick.
God is my strength, unfailing, quick.

God is my all, I know no fear,
Since God and Love and Truth are here."[3]

Within two weeks from the time he had memorized
and affirmed over and over, daily, these words of faith,
this man was feeling better as the pain had diminished
and he was able to walk more easily. Thereafter, he daily
improved so much that within three months' time he was
able to dig in his garden and again became active far
beyond his fondest dreams. Gradually he was freed of
the white, stiff arthritic fingers and of the painful neuritis throughout the body. Thirty years later, at the age
of 77, this man was still enjoying good health.

FAITH IS BELIEF

The 16th-century German physician Paracelsus is reported to have said that faith would cure all disease.

Why are words of faith so powerful? Because faith is
that which is believed. Faith is a deep inner conviction,
a state of certainty, a state of super-assurance. *When you
feel deeply, you liberate an enormous amount of energy!*

Your thinking is your faith. *Whatever you are firm
about in your thinking, you have faith in. Through that
firm belief you release a super-atomic energy into your
system to work for or against you, depending upon the
nature of your belief.* Faith is a fountain of energy within
man, tapped by his faith thinking.

Dr. Phineas P. Quimby is considered by many to be
the founder of mental and spiritual healing in America.

3. Hannah More Kohaus, *Prayer of Faith* (Unity Village, MO:
Unity School of Christianity).

While healing so many of his New England neighbors during the 19th-century, Dr. Quimby developed a simple method for arousing the healing power of faith in his patients.

When sick people visited him for a "mind cure," Dr. Quimby would sit quietly and talk to them about their beliefs, gradually changing their deep-seated negative convictions as he explained the origin of disease as being within their own wrong beliefs. When those beliefs were changed, the patients were healed.

In *The Quimby Manuscripts*[4] he explains what disease is:

"A belief is what I call a disease. It is false reasoning. The life of disease is in the person who believes it. Disease is a mental condition, an invention of man. Disease is in beliefs. Correct your opinions and you will be free of disease."

Explaining why and how we can be free of disease, he writes:

"The mind is the cause of disease and has equal power in overcoming it. The mind does not act of itself, but is acted upon by thoughts within and opinions without. Whatever opinion we put into a thing, that we can take out of it. The mind is made up of ideas held in mind. *Concentration upon just one single principle will change the mind magically and cause it to rise in confidence above many of its previous beliefs and fears.*"

Again, emphasizing the power of one's beliefs upon the body, he writes:

4. Phineas P. Quimby, *The Quimby Manuscripts*, ed. Horatio W. Dresser (New York: The Julian Press, Inc., 1961).

"I found that my thoughts were one thing and my *beliefs* another. If I really *believed* a thing, the effect would follow whether I was thinking of it or not."

BELIEF HEALS

The greatest Healer that ever walked this earth certainly would have agreed with Dr. Quimby. Jesus constantly turned His followers' attention to the power found in that word "believe."

"All things are possible to him that believeth." (Mark 9:23)

"And when he was come into the house, the blind men came to him, and Jesus saith unto them, Believe ye that I am able to do this? They say unto him, Yes, Lord. Then touched he their eyes saying, According to your faith be it done unto you. And their eyes were opened." (Matthew 9:28-30)

"O thou of little faith! Why didst thou not believe?" (Matthew 14:31)

"Be not faithless, but believing." (John 20:27)

"And these signs shall accompany them that believe: in my name shall they cast out demons . . . they shall lay hands on the sick, and they shall recover." (Mark 16:17, 18)

When his disciples asked Jesus why they had failed in healing certain cases, his terse reply was:

"Because of your unbelief." (Matthew 17:20)

At another time when they pressed Him to give them the secret of His power, He explained:

"This is the work of God, that ye believe on him whom
He hath sent." (John 6:29)

Does this word "believe" truly have the healing power
Jesus suggested? Indeed, it does!

A 50-year-old woman had been pronounced incurable
by her doctors. She had an internal disease which apparently had spread so throughout her body that an
operation could not stop it. Seeking out the solace of a
spiritual counselor, it was suggested that she dwell on the
word "believe" and affirm it over and over. Her constant
refrain became, "Yes Lord, I believe You can and will
heal me." In moments of doubt, she joined the father of
the epileptic boy of Jesus' time in declaring, "I believe;
help thou my unbelief." (Mark 9:24)

Within two weeks she realized that she was receiving
a deep spiritual healing. As her inner faith faculty was
awakened, it gave her the courage to hold to the word
"believe" until a gradual healing completely restored her
body to perfect health. She proved that whatever you
believe in, you serve and are served by!

FAITH WORKS EITHER WAY

This matter of faith or belief works equally strong
either way. Sick folks have faith—plenty of it—but in the
wrong thing. *Your attention is your faith. Whatever gets
your attention gets your faith. Whatever you give your
attention, you have faith in. Whatever you are deeply
convinced about, you have faith in. Whatever you expect and prepare for, you have faith in.*

There once was a man who often said: "Everyone in
my family dies at the age of 65. It 'runs in the family.'

My father died at that age, so did my mother. My aunts, uncles, and several cousins all died at that age, and I will too." This man was deeply convinced about this. He was firm in his mind about it. He gave his full attention to this belief. He had faith in it. He expected it.

In his expectations he went even further: "I will die from a stroke attended by high blood pressure and heart trouble because everyone in my family has died that way. By the time I am 61, I will have my first heart attack and stroke. After that 'nature will take its course' and it will just be a matter of time."

Right on schedule at the age of 61, he had his first heart attack and a light stroke. He then retired from his job and within the next few years continued to have light strokes and heart trouble. Again, right on time, during his sixty-fifth year he died from another stroke and heart attack, in spite of the finest medical care.

At the time this man had begun to make these decrees ten years earlier, he had been in fine health. But, according to his faith, it was done unto him!

FAITH HEARS AND SEES

The interesting thing about your words of faith is that they are always creating or dissolving, according to what you have faith in—either health or disease. When words of faith have been spoken to large tumors, these false growths have been known to melt away. When words of faith have been spoken to paralyzed organs, they have been restored to life. Yet the same power of faith has equal authority to destroy one's health, if used destructively.

A woman kept attending healing lectures and repeatedly placed her name in the church's prayer ministry to receive healing prayers. Yet she remained as sick as ever, and could not understand why.

Investigation revealed that she kept talking about her ill health, kept listening to descriptions of all the health problems "enjoyed" by a neurotic neighbor, and generally immersed her attention in the subject of disease. Through her faith and attention to ill health, she kept it manifesting. Her faith was an irresistible force, but for illness instead of for wholeness.

All the prayers in the world cannot heal you when you still turn your attention to and accept ill health as "necessary" for you. Your attention has result-getting power, so be careful what you give your attention to. Your attention *is* your faith.

The fact that your mind power of faith at the pineal gland is located between the ears and eyes has special significance: It indicates that what you listen to with your ears and see with your eyes, you have faith in and will manifest in your life. The fact that the pineal gland is affected by light is symbolic. Your faith is affected by mental and spiritual enlightenment. When you are trying to see and hear only the highest and best, thus expressing faith in connection with some situation, person, or diagnosis, it is good to decree: "LET THERE BE LIGHT." Also, that is the time to call on the super-intelligence of the Christ Mind located at the crown of the head: "I HAVE FAITH THAT I AM UPLIFTED AND UPHELD BY THE CHRIST MIND. NOTHING CAN DISTURB THE CALM PEACE OF MY SOUL."

People who misuse their imagination to image all kinds of evil appearances often have trouble with the mind power of imagination between the eyes. Misuse of faith, which is located level with the eyes, can cause much trouble in the vision and eyesight. Faith is the perceiving or seeing power of the mind, and when we persist in seeing evil appearances rather than having faith in God's goodness, our vision of evil naturally affects the eyes. A person's eyes will often get out of focus because he is perceiving evil instead of good; or because his faith is mixed, partly good and partly negative, producing a mixed, unfocused result.

One's hearing is also often affected by misuse of the mind power of faith. Paul pointed out to the Romans: "Faith cometh by hearing." (Romans 10:17) Simon Peter was the disciple who metaphysically symbolizes faith, and Simon means "hearing."

Previously healthy children were placed in an atmosphere of tension and hate, following the divorce of their parents. Immediately their eyes and ears were affected.

In another unhappy family, where the children were required to listen to negative radio and television news reports while eating their meals, their ears and eyes were also severely affected with health problems. In still another family, the parents fussed at their children while they ate, criticizing their table manners, often sending them away from the table in tears and hungry. These children also developed severe ear and eye diseases, which faded away when they grew up and escaped the inharmony of their parents' home.

FAITH BRINGS WOMAN BACK FROM DEATH

The faith center located in the pineal gland seems to open the mind of man to spiritual faith, through which all things are possible. Merely affirming the activity of this super-power of faith will quicken it in your mind, body and affairs, often producing remarkable results quickly. Furthermore, someone else having faith for the one needing it can activate that person to wholeness and health again, as proved by the following experience of a housewife:

"I was notified along with the rest of my family that an aunt was not expected to live more than 24 hours. She had been suffering from ill health for several years and no one was surprised. However, for financial reasons, it was not possible for me to get to her side right away, so I sat down alone most of the day, and talked to my sick aunt about having faith as though I were right there with her, though I was 250 miles away. I called her name and said to her over and over, 'Believe and you shall receive a healing.'

"I sensed that she was afraid of death, so as I called her name, I told her there was nothing to fear; that life went on; that death was like going from one room to another; that she could be free to go on if she wished. But if she wanted to stay with us all here, she could do so if she would have faith. Over and over I said to her, 'I HAVE FAITH IN GOD'S LIFE WITHIN YOU. THIS APPEARANCE OF DEATH HAS NO POWER. IT IS NOTHING. THERE IS NOTHING IN EXISTENCE BUT LIFE, LIFE, LIFE!'

"My aunt remained in a coma for the next 36 hours. At that time I finally arrived at the hospital. When I entered her room, she opened her eyes, called my name and said, 'I knew you would come to help me. I have faith, I am not afraid.' Then she sank back into unconsciousness.

"During the next three days, she slipped back and forth from consciousness to unconsciousness. In the process she talked about her family. There seemed to be problems concerning her children that deeply depressed her. I assured her there was nothing to fear; to have faith in the goodness of God to resolve everything. Though she remained alive, doctors held out no hope for her recovery.

"Then about noon on the third day she seemed to die: There was no heartbeat, no blood pressure and her breathing stopped. Doctors and nurses worked diligently to get medication into the veins to revive her. As they worked, I stood at a distance and kept my eyes on her face and forehead, which were the only areas of her body not covered. I remembered that the faith center in man is found in the head between the ears and eyes. I reasoned that if I spoke words of faith to her, she would 'hear' them with her inner ear of faith. Over and over I said to her silently 'Have faith, Auntie. Your life is God's life. I believe and you believe, and there is nothing to fear.'

"Finally she responded to treatment and was revived. Later when she was stronger, but was still drifting back and forth between being conscious and unconscious, she insisted on talking. Weakly she told me to tell her husband not to be afraid for her to go on to the other side; that she had been there, had seen her father, brother, a sister-in-law, and a family doctor (all of whom were dead). She said they were happy and busy, that a pretty light shone around them. She then described the beauty of the next plane with its vivid flowers, grass, and gardens. She said that while there she had been able to walk and run again. (She had not been able to walk in four years.)

"My aunt then stated that although everything on the other side was peaceful and beautiful, and even though her many friends and relatives there seemed happy, she had decided to stay here with her family who still needed her.

"Later when she was recovering nicely, she did not remember having said these things. She did get well, helped several members of her family through severe illnesses, and reared her children. Her health improved greatly after this near fatal illness, and she had more peace of mind than previously.

"This experience convinced me that words of faith can unlock the door to healing."

Life never ceases. Man simply loses his hold on it by losing his faith in it. Restored faith brings restored life. These people proved it.

WORDS OF FAITH CURE THE INCURABLE

Have faith in the power of your mind to penetrate and release the energy that is pent up in the atoms of your body. You may be astounded at the response!

A young woman was informed by her doctor that she had an incurable disease, that a series of tests would have to be made to determine what treatment was needed, but that surgery was probably her only hope.

Frightened by this diagnosis, this young woman hurried over to see a spiritual counselor, who talked with her about the healing power of faith. Together they affirmed, "I HAVE UNSHAKABLE FAITH IN THE PERFECT OUTCOME OF EVERY SITUATION IN MY LIFE, FOR GOD IS IN ABSOLUTE CONTROL." Together they also affirmed that nothing but God's good was present and active in this woman's body; that only good could be seen in her body; that only good could be found; that only good would come forth from this experience.

A few days later, further tests revealed clear X-rays! What had previously appeared was no longer there. Since there was nothing foreign to remove, there was no need for surgery.

Sometimes such a conviction of healing can be reached immediately. At other times it takes persistent effort for hours, days, even weeks, before faith's healing power has been sufficiently activated and released. At such times one should affirm, "I HAVE FAITH THAT I AM CURABLE. I HAVE FAITH THAT GOD'S INDWELLING POWER IS HEALING ME NOW. I HAVE FAITH THAT ALL THINGS ARE

WORKING TOGETHER FOR GOOD IN MY MIND, BODY AND LIFE
NOW."

Jesus placed special emphasis upon persistency in
faith, showing through parable and teaching that success in healing comes to those who do not give up. Faith
works through patience as well as through the feeling
nature of love.

We have often heard it said that faith without works
is dead. (James 2:17) Well, *faith without nerve to continue in it is dead, too!*

When there is something "foreign" in the body, it is
an indication that there is something "foreign" in the
mind that needs to be dissolved. A *"growth" in the body
is an indication that there is need for growth in one's
spiritual understanding; growth and deeper development of one's mind power of faith.*

AN INTERNAL "GROWTH" HEALED

Two women were told by their doctors that they had
internal growths. One of them went immediately to her
lawyer and made a will. She said, "I am terribly sick. I
know I'm going to die." She prepared for death and it
obediently appeared.

The other woman said, "I know I am God's child and
He loves me. There can be no limitation of God's life in
me. I am going to look on what the doctor calls a
'growth' as opportunity to grow in faith. Anything that
happens to me has to be for good. I have faith that God
is in charge of this experience in my spiritual growth."

She prayed for her health, kept declaring she was a
wonderful child of God, and had faith in His healing
power actively at work within her. A month later when

she returned for a checkup, the growth was much smaller. Eventually it disappeared entirely! Meanwhile her faith faculty had expanded immeasurably and proved a tremendous blessing in other phases of her life as well.

Healing is first a "growth" in consciousness. Healing results as a growth out of old limited beliefs into an expanded faith, and the goodness of God is achieved. The faith faculty of the mind is developed in much the same way that the muscles of the body are developed. Persistent affirmation concentrates the mental energies and dissolves all barriers. Affirmation releases the pent-up energies in mind and body, and frees them to produce healthy results.

HOW TO DEVELOP YOUR FAITH

Jesus tapped the universal mind power of faith, and one healing after another followed his spoken words of faith. What He did He claimed we might do also.

Faith is the result of many affirmations. After studying the success secrets of 500 of this country's leading millionaires, Napoleon Hill gave their secret techniques for developing faith in his book, *Think and Grow Rich.*[5]

"Faith is a state of mind, which may be induced or created by affirmation . . . Repetition of orders to your subconscious mind is the only known method of voluntary development of the emotion of faith."

5. Napoleon Hill, *Think and Grow Rich* (Rev. ed.; New York: Hawthorn Publishing Co., 1966). Copyrighted by The Napoleon Hill Foundation.

But as the famous Scottish philosopher, Thomas Carlyle, pointed out: "Conviction is useless until converted to action." Or as Ralph Waldo Emerson put it: "The law of nature is: 'Do the thing and you have the power; but they who do not do the thing have not the power.'"

The Greeks believed that health was an entity that would come by being called. Just as Jesus "called" his 12 disciples, you can begin developing your 12 mind powers by gently "calling" them, giving them your attention. Your mind powers are like people. They can be praised and blessed into much activity, but they rebel against force, so "easy does it." Gently and lovingly begin to give them your attention and recognition and they will respond, but in their own time and way. They will not be forced, rushed, or dictated to.

Your mind power of faith, located in the pineal gland, between the eyes and ears, is one of your most interior mind powers. Since it is located in the area of the forehead, within the seat of your conscious mind, this indicates that you can begin consciously and deliberately developing your miracle-working faith through your words of faith.

In developing your mind power of faith begin by first centering your attention at the crown of the head, invoking the super-intelligence of the Christ Mind. Affirm: "I AM THE CHRIST MIND, I AM, I AM, I AM. I AM LETTING THE SUPER-INTELLIGENCE OF THE CHRIST MIND NOW EXPRESS THROUGH ME. I AM, I AM, I AM.."

This releases the dynamic energy of the Christ Mind (the true idea of God) to gently flow down into the conscious mind at the forehead, and then to flow down into the subconscious regions of the heart and abdominal area of the body. Sweep your attention from the top of your head to the tip of your toes with these affirmations. This mental act gives your whole body the benefits of the increased activity of the Christ Mind.

Then center your attention in the area of the faith faculty between the eyes in the forehead and "call" your mind power of faith into activity.

"FAITH, FAITH, FAITH. I HAVE FAITH IN GOD. I HAVE FAITH IN PEOPLE. I HAVE FAITH IN THINGS."

"I HAVE FAITH IN THE HEALING POWER OF GOD AS IT WORKS MIGHTILY IN ME NOW. I HAVE FAITH THAT ALL THINGS ARE NOW WORKING TOGETHER FOR MY GOOD AND I AM WORKING WITH THEM IN THE WISDOM AND POWER OF SPIRIT. I HAVE FAITH IN THE PERFECT OUTCOME OF EVERY SITUATION IN MY LIFE, FOR GOD IS IN ABSOLUTE CONTROL. MY FAITH NOW MAKES ME WHOLE!"

Dwell often upon Bible promises that express faith, such as, "Thy faith hath made thee whole." (Luke 17:19)

Again, sweep your body from head to toe with some of these affirmations of faith. Remember also to relax and breathe deeply as you "call" your mind powers into activity, preferably by lying on a slant board in a relaxed position. During your quiet times when you are developing your mind powers, relax and release all outer appearances in your life, as you turn within to your mind powers which love you, and wish to help you by going to work for you. There is nothing difficult or complex about developing them. Your mind powers have been patiently longing to be noticed and activated in a constructive way. As you do so quietly, lovingly, gently they will gladly respond and a gradual transformation will be felt in your mind, body, and affairs. It is then that you will know what the great apostle, Paul, meant when he said, "Be ye transformed by the renewing of your mind." (Romans 12:2)

As you speak forth words of faith, consciously developing first your faith faculty and later your other mind powers, you may wish to meditate often upon the wisdom of the Persian philosopher, Zoroaster. His words will assure you of the result-getting power you are releasing.

> One may heal with Holiness.
> One may heal with the law.
> One may heal with knife.
> One may heal with herbs.
> One may heal with the Holy Word: This one it is, that will best drive away sickness from the body of the faithful.
> For this is the best healing of all remedies.

Your healing power of

STRENGTH

— 3 —

During a California earthquake, cripples who had not walked in years suddenly fled. During World War II, as the bombs fell in Europe, the same thing happened to those who had thought they were totally incapacitated.

More recently a businessman was ill with a kink in his back. In bed unable to move, he affirmed strength and healing for himself. Suddenly as his wife yelled "Fire, fire!" he quickly jumped out of bed, rushed into the kitchen and repaired an ignited fuse, before realizing his prayers had now been answered.

We usually think of strength as a vital essence that flows throughout the body, but *strength is also a mind power.* This mind power is located in the loins at the small of the back, between the hipbones and ribs as shown in Figure 3-1.

These people had unwittingly tapped this mind power of strength and when faced with an emergency, this mind power was suddenly activated, releasing deeper

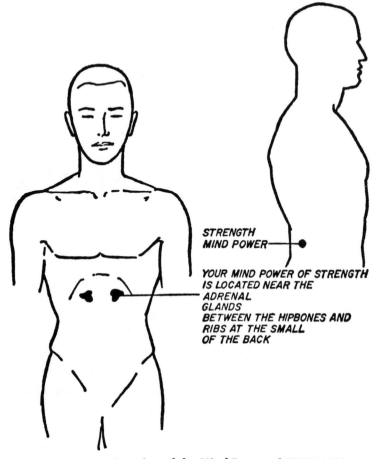

STRENGTH
MIND POWER

YOUR MIND POWER OF STRENGTH
IS LOCATED NEAR THE
ADRENAL
GLANDS
BETWEEN THE HIPBONES AND
RIBS AT THE SMALL
OF THE BACK

Figure 3–1.   Location of the Mind Power of STRENGTH.

levels of energy to meet the demand of the moment. The
mind power of strength has the power to do this because
it is located in the area of the adrenal glands in the loins.
These are the glands of emotion, equipped to meet suddenly the emergencies of life by quickly releasing increased energy and vitality into the body.

CENTER OF STRENGTH IS THREE-FOLD

From ancient times it has been an established truth that the center of strength in the body is located at the small of the back. Job said, "His strength is in his loins." (Job 40:16) Solomon's description of a worthy woman was "She girdeth her loins with strength." (Proverbs 31:17)

Actually strength is three-fold: On the *physical plane,* strength is power, energy, vitality, and freedom from weakness in the body. On the *mental plane,* strength is the ability to achieve, to be a leader, to be expert in one's field of work. It is freedom from mental or emotional weakness. On the *spiritual plane,* strength is steadfastness to the belief in good, persistence in expecting it, and the ability to withstand temptation, or the refusal to settle for less than the best in one's life experiences. When one is tempted to do so, it stirs up that deeper strength to dwell on an ancient saying: *"The highest is the nearest."*

Strength is the ability to keep on keeping on, despite negative conditions in one's body or affairs. Strength is not physical violence or mental force. It is a quiet energy that is stirred up by man's faith in the good. As strength is activated, it flows into every department of one's life — physical, mental, spiritual — producing remarkable improvements there.

The word "strength" means "to endure," "to persist." There is an old Italian proverb, "He conquers who endures." Ancient philosophers taught that the way to eliminate evil from one's world and from one's own body was to perpetually declare, "THERE IS NO STRENGTH OR POWER BUT IN GOD THE GOOD."

The fact that strength is far more than just physical

energy, which affects one's health, is shown in the statistic that between 50 and 75 percent of the people who seek medical treatment have nothing organically wrong with them. Their lack of physical strength is but an indication of the need for mental, emotional, and spiritual strength.

AN EXECUTIVE HEALED A SERIOUS AILMENT IN HIS BACK

When a person has gotten "down in his back," it is an indication that he first got "down in his thinking." The mind power of strength located in the small of the back is directly connected with the faith faculty in the temples through the nerve system of the spinal cord.

As your mind power of faith develops and your ability to hear and see the good with the ears and eyes of faith unfolds, you then need strength as steadfastness and stability to carry forth that higher vision of good. Emotionally unstable people should work to develop the mind power of strength which would give them the stability for which they long.

Many people stir up their faith; they perceive a healing as possible for them, but they do not manifest it in the body *because they do not persist.* They need to affirm strength and steadfastness to see things through. (The metaphysical link between faith and strength is shown in the fact that Peter and Andrew were brothers. Peter is the disciple who symbolizes faith and Andrew is the disciple who symbolizes strength.)

A Texas oilman had for several months been under a severe financial strain and became very ill with his back and kidneys. The pain was so severe that he could not stand up and had to be helped in and out of bed. Because of the kidney infection, he had very high fever and his doctors wanted him hospitalized.

However, this oilman and his wife had both studied the 12 powers of the mind. They knew that financial burdens were the cause of this back trouble. They had faith that the only permanent solution to this illness was to call forth increased strength from the mind power located in the small of the back, from which the pain was coming.

Because of the pain, weakness and fever, this man felt unable to make affirmations for himself. As he lay quietly saying to the pain, "Relax, let go," his wife went into her study to pray. Remembering the words of Isaiah, "Lift up thy voice with strength," (Isaiah 40:9) she began affirming for her husband: "YOU CAST ALL FINANCIAL BURDENS ON THE CHRIST WITHIN AND YOU GO FREE. I BAPTIZE YOUR MIND POWER OF STRENGTH IN THE NAME OF THE FATHER, THE SON, AND THE HOLY SPIRIT. YOU ARE NOW FREED FROM ALL BURDENS — PHYSICAL, MENTAL, FINANCIAL."

After working an hour in prayer and affirmation for her husband, she got a sense of peace. Knowing that *peace is the forerunner of healing,* she realized her prayers were being answered. Two hours later all pain and fever had left her husband. From that point on he gained in strength daily. As they continued to affirm strength, his financial affairs became orderly and he was able to meet the financial obligations which had earlier been a burden to both mind and body.

HOW A DOMESTIC FINANCIAL
PROBLEM WAS HEALED

A housewife got "down in her back" while her house was being redecorated. Upon learning that financial problems are often reflected as back problems, she suddenly realized the source of her back trouble. Her husband had turned the whole decoration project over to her, and she had been unduly concerned about its financial cost as well as about other details. After she began affirming "strength" not only was her back healed, but also all financial details became orderly, too. Her husband decided his business was doing well enough to draw a bonus from it to cover redecoration expenses, so that no financial burden was incurred.

STRENGTH IS RELATED TO SUBSTANCE

Strength is related to substance. Financial problems can drain the strength center in the body. You can meet financial demands successfully and keep them from draining you physically and emotionally, if you will affirm that you have the strength to meet them victoriously. Then sit down and give thanks[1] and bless[2] what you have. In this way you will make connection with the mind power of strength. As it is activated, abundant strength will well up within you, overflowing into your affairs as abundant ideas and opportunities which will

---

1. See the chapters, "The Healing Law of Praise" in *The Dynamic Laws of Healing*, and "The Miracle Law of Prosperity" in *The Millionaire Moses*, both books by Catherine Ponder.

2. See the chapter, "Ancient Secret for Happy Living" in her book, *The Prosperity Secrets of the Ages*.

manifest as increased supply. Then, you will know what Hannah meant in her song of thanksgiving when she chanted, "They that stumbled are girded with strength." (I Samuel 2:4)

EMOTIONAL BURDENS CAUSE BACK TROUBLES

Since your mind power of strength is in the abdominal region, this indicates that it is located in the center of your subconscious mind or emotional nature which functions from the abdominal part of the body. When a person has trouble with his back, it is an indication that it may not have been his recent conscious thinking that caused the trouble; but it may be the subconscious belief in burdens—his own or another's—which have accumulated in his deep feelings over a long period of time. Edgar Cayce's readings on the ancient wisdom regarding the glands revealed that the adrenals were the storehouse of one's emotional *karma* in the body. This could also explain certain health problems in that area.

The adrenal glands, in which the mind power of strength is located, are situated on both sides of the abdomen, astride and back of the kidneys. Two in number and about as big as the end of one's finger, the adrenals are known as the "glands of combat" and struggle, because they quickly respond to rage, anger, fear. In times of emergency, their secretion is stimulated.

Since they are "glands of combat," the emotions stirred up by continual inharmony in one's life affect that area of the body. Cancer is common in the small of the back among people who have long lived with secret inharmony in their lives. Suppressed anger adversely affects this area, too.

A successful businessman had suffered in secret from the jealousy of his possessive wife for years. To all appearances they were a happy, church-going couple. But behind closed doors, their lives were filled with continual strife.

After carrying this emotional burden over many years, this man finally developed cancer at the small of the back, which spread to the entire lower abdominal region. Although his wife asked for prayers for her husband from various healers and church groups, it was too late. The years of emotional combat between them had done their work in this man's body, and he no longer had the physical or emotional strength to combat her jealousy. He finally got his freedom from the burdens of this life through death. Though his wife's prayers were not answered, his doubtless were, through the release that death gave him.

The adrenal glands, in which the strength center is located, are closely connected with the sympathetic nervous system. Just how important they are to the body is shown by the fact that if they are removed, death results. The adrenals react strongly to unhealthy mental and emotional conditions. They are temperamental glands that react to one's jealousies, hates, fears, struggles for success, power or position. Every strong emotional reaction causes them to release extra reserves of adrenal secretion; thus, excessive emotional demands exhaust them and lead to death, as in the case of the successful businessman. The adrenal glands are the fighters of the body. When highly emotional people overwork their adrenal glands, lack of strength follows, attended by exhaustion and even death.

The physical potency of the adrenal glands' secretion is shown in the fact that adrenaline is injected into the heart to revive dying patients.

A DRAMATIC CASE OF ADRENAL
STIMULATION SAVING A LIFE

A nurse was attending a patient who had been in a diabetic coma. Awaiting the doctor's arrival, she was trying to keep him conscious as she gave him an orange juice mixture. But he was unable to swallow it. Realizing he needed this nourishment for minimum strength to remain alive, she suddenly felt impelled to slap the patient, and did so! The startled patient quickly swallowed the juice before losing consciousness. Later he revived, and was sitting up when the doctor arrived.

Amazed, the doctor later asked the nurse what she had done to save this patient and she told him. He replied, "That was the best thing you could have done. The body gives off adrenaline when one is either afraid or angry. By slapping the patient, you made him angry. His adrenal glands then became active and gave him the strength needed to swallow the juice, the contents of which saved his life."

In emotionally healthy people, the adrenal glands are well equipped to face emergencies and release extra supplies of energy and strength into the body as the need arises. A person who is rightly using his mind power of strength conserves his vital substance of strength and does not waste it in emotional dissipation caused by negative emotions.

HOW STRENGTH IS DEVELOPED

Sometimes you do not actually have an ache or pain in the back. But when you have become burdened by your own troubles or have taken on someone else's problems, you get a tired, uncomfortable feeling in the back. You feel weak, ineffective, discouraged, unable to see things through. That is the time to affirm: "I AM STRONG IN THE LORD AND IN THE POWER OF HIS MIGHT. MY YOKE IS EASY AND MY BURDEN IS LIGHT. I FACE THE WORLD STRONG, FREE AND UNAFRAID."

As the wife of the oilman discovered, you can literally "baptize" the mind power of strength with words of strength. This activates mental and physical strength to meet the need of the moment, to persist, to see things through.

Remember, too, that the heaviest burdens anyone ever bears are the burdens of his own negative thoughts and words. These heavy, unpleasant burdensome thoughts include such debris as suspicion, doubt, fear, ingratitude, self-pity, hurt feelings, impatience, jealousy, envy, condemnation, revenge, injustice, bitterness.

When a person does not know how to neutralize these negative emotions, it is then that serious diseases develop in the strength center at the small of the back.

Very definite changes occur in mind and body when one dwells upon the mind power of "strength." True strength comes from meditating upon strength. Every word has a quality that sympathetically relates it to an idea innate in the mind of man. When that word is released, it radiates an energy that contracts and expands the body cells. *There is power in this word to increase further strength!*

Strength is developed through sustained effort, rather than through spurts and flashes of effort, which only produce spurts and flashes of energy.

When you persistently affirm "strength," those words call forth the deeper levels of strength stored in the cells of the body, especially in the strength center at the small of the back. Continued affirmations of strength act as an invigorating tonic, releasing strength in the brain centers of each of your 12 mind powers. It is in these 12 vital brain centers that energy is stored for that particular mind power. Your affirmations awaken and release that vital energy and as that energy is released, your body is renewed.

I once knew a lady who looked 20 years younger than she actually was. She worked long hours in a demanding profession; yet she was never sick, had tremendous energy, and met both physical and emotional demands that would have overwhelmed the average person. Her secret? She regularly retired to her bedroom at the end of each day, relaxed her body, and "baptized" her 12 mind powers, especially calling forth "strength."

As you deliberately activate your 12 mind powers, releasing their energy into the entire body, you will find chronic diseases passing away. First, the surface mental and emotional causes of those diseases will be dissolved. Next, you will cease fearing or talking about those diseases. Then as you persist in your affirmations, the deeper mental and emotional causes of the disease are penetrated, broken up, and rise to the surface of your emotions, after which they pass from mind and body forever. [3]

SPINE AND BACK REFLECT THE WILL

The spinal cord is filled with nerve centers that branch out to every part of the body. By affirming strength, you release your strength to flow freely along the nerves and penetrate every cell. As strength flows up and down the

3. See Chapter 12, "Chemicalization, A Healing Process" in *The Dynamic Laws of Healing.*

spinal column, penetrating the various areas of the body, you feel uplifted, revitalized, renewed. Sometimes when your mind power of strength is developed in the small of the back, your spinal cord becomes very sensitive, as it becomes accustomed to the increased energy flowing through it. At such times it is good to affirm: "ORDERLY RENEWAL, ADJUSTMENT, AND RESTORATION ARE NOW TAKING PLACE IN MY MIND, BODY, AND AFFAIRS."

Spines can be straightened, paralysis healed, muscles restored, and nerves revitalized as one affirms: "NEW STRENGTH IS FLOWING FREELY TO EVERY PART OF MY BEING NOW. I AM RENEWED IN SPIRIT, SOUL, AND BODY."

Although the mind power of strength is found in the small of the back, misuse of strength, or lack of strength, is reflected through various parts of the body. For instance, the shoulders symbolize responsibility. When responsibility becomes burdensome; when it is either grudgingly accepted, unwillingly borne, or accompanied by self-pity, it shows forth as health problems in the shoulders.

A FALSE SENSE OF RESPONSIBILITY CAN CAUSE PHYSICAL BREAKDOWN

When one is properly developing the mind power of strength, one realizes that responsibilities are not a burden, but they are soul-expanding when rightly assumed and lovingly met. Use of the following affirmations helps: "I NO LONGER RESENT MY RESPONSIBILITIES. THEY ARE EXPANDING MY GOOD IN EVERY PHASE OF MY WORLD. MY YOKE IS EASY AND MY BURDENS ARE LIGHT."

When we bear burdens that should not be ours to bear, it is usually reflected as trouble in the shoulders. A businessman had for many years been serving in a place of great financial responsibility for a certain civic organization. Often he had said, "This organization could not survive if it were not for my financial help." In due time he developed a gnawing pain between his shoulders which medical or chiropractic treatment seemed unable to alleviate, except temporarily.

Finally metaphysical study revealed the shoulders as the area of responsibility in the body, and this man realized he had assumed a false sense of responsibility about this organization and its financial obligations. He resigned his post, released this organization emotionally, relaxed more, began to travel and enjoy life generally. With the release of false responsibility, came release from the former pain between the shoulders. It faded away completely.

A frustrated divorcee took all kinds of treatments to lose weight. Invariably she would lose weight everywhere except through her shoulders, which might have belonged to a football player. She also suffered physical ailments there. This woman was always fighting with her family, assuming financial responsibilities which they did not wish her to bear. She constantly meddled in other people's business. Her false sense of responsibility reflected as health problems in her shoulders.

A widow was heavily burdened with an elderly mother and two grown sons who drained her financially and emotionally. Though still a young woman, she suffered from arthritis of the back and shoulders. At a time when she was thousands of dollars in debt, she took up the study of practical Christianity, and through it began to develop an inner strength she had never previously known. Often she affirmed from David's song of praise: "GOD IS MY STRENGTH AND MY POWER, AND HE MAKETH MY WAY PERFECT." (II Sam. 22:33)

As she also practiced releasing her burdens mentally,

vast improvement came. The elderly mother passed on peacefully; her adult children finally got jobs; she was guided into a new field of work which she had long wished to do. Because of its more lucrative compensation, she was able to begin meeting her financial challenges victoriously. As she was freed of false responsibilities, the arthritis gradually faded from the back and shoulder area, and she resumed good health.

While the shoulders symbolize responsibility, the hips symbolize individual independence, free will and self-support. The shoulders, which help to form the walls of the chest cavity that contains the heart and lungs, are closely akin to the spiritual nature of life and are counterbalanced by the hips.

The hip bones help to form the pelvic basin that supports the generative organs, which are closely associated with the formation of the personal, physical life. The hipbone also contains the socket into which the head of the thighbone fits. This joint makes it possible for a man to sit down and to move around. When a person selfishly depends too completely on others to support him, he cripples his own abilities and manifests health problems in the hips and small of the back.

The spine and back show forth one's will. We often refer to a person of strength and courage as one "having backbone." People with dominating wills often have spine and back trouble. Jacob's hip was thrown out of place by the angel with whom he wrestled, because he wanted his own way. To avoid this, affirm, "I AM A TOWER OF STRENGTH WITHIN AND WITHOUT BECAUSE I AM ESTABLISHED IN DIVINE STRENGTH. NOT MY WILL, BUT THINE BE DONE."

Then rejoice that you are self-supporting. Rejoice that you can stand on your own feet. Rejoice that no false condition has any power over you.

GOOD IS ANOTHER NAME FOR STRENGTH

The act of affirming the good releases the highest energy of which the human mind is capable. Emma Curtis Hopkins explained that "good" is another name for "strength" in her book *Scientific Christian Mental Practice*.[4]

"Another name of the Good we are seeking is 'strength.' All things look for strength. They love strength. The baby laughs at every waft of strength through its little frame. The insect runs and rolls with speechless delight at every quiver of new strength. The Good it seeks is strength unlimited. It wants free, boundless strength. So do you.

"If you name your Good as unlimited strength, you will feel free and strong at once. As you look at some feeble woman, and think further that the Good she is seeking is unlimited strength, she will let her mind shine with yours. She has felt that unconsciously. She will feel strength consciously. Everything you tell the omnipotent Truth to, that its strength is God and God is its strength, will rise and be strong; and you will be stronger the more you proclaim the irresistible idea which all creation feels."

As a metaphysical healer, Mrs. Hopkins explained the various phases of strength in her book.

"The first strength of mind is the strength to endure . . . A good man may seem to be very frail, but he will live on and on where others, more robust looking, would falter, because goodness is the substance in man which endures. . . .

"The second strength is the . . . strength of fearlessness. It comes to you by always believing everything is

4. Published by DeVorss & Co., Marina del Rey, CA, p.20.

good which seems good, and that everyone is good who seems good. *Let your conscious thoughts and words be according to the Good.* This will give you a young and fearless look in the face, and keep you vigorous. You will find that anyone who is full of certainty that what seems good is good, has a young look . . . Youth is kept by refusing to believe evil of people or things."

Another metaphysical healer once related her simple method for clearing up all kinds of burdens in mind, body, and affairs as:

"Some twenty-five years ago, when I began the study of Truth, and began developing as a healer, only one mighty thought remained with me at the close of my first six months of study. That thought was: *'Only the good is real.'*

"I have practiced holding to this thought for myself and others, almost without a break during these twenty-five years, and I have witnessed hundreds of demonstrations in healing, supply and human relations as I have held to this one mighty thought: *'Only the good is real.'*"

Do you wonder why the thought of good has such power? It is because *the thought of good releases strength into the spiritual, mental, and physical levels of your life.* The thought of good dissolves all kinds of beliefs in burdens that may have settled in your back, kidneys, hips, or shoulder areas. This thought of good dissolves suspicion, doubt, fear, ingratitude, self-pity, grudges, sadness, hurt feelings, impatience, hatred, condemnation, revenge and bitterness. All kinds of negative thoughts that cause burdens in man's mind, body, and affairs can be cleared up with this simple statement: *Only the good is real.* One healer proved it. So can you!

AN OCCULT SECRET TO RELEASE
GOOD FOR YOURSELF

Here is an occult secret that has been quietly known and used for centuries:

The word "good" is synonymous with the word "God." When you speak forth the word "*good*," you are releasing a divine power. The word "good" is creative. Good is created as fast as good thoughts and words are released. When you speak forth the word "good," you evolve, stir up, and release great good to manifest.

The word "good" is self-increasing. When you speak forth words of good, you not only create good, but also that good continues to create more good! It is self-multiplying. Thus, by speaking words of good, you first create and then increase the strength within your mind, body, and affairs. Good is another name for strength — spiritual, mental and physical.

You call upon the mind power of strength within when you pronounce everything good. To troublesome situations, personalities, financial problems, as well as to troublesome aches, pains, and burdens that appear in the small of the back declare: "I PRONOUNCE YOU GOOD." *When you muster up the strength to pronounce negative situations and diagnoses as good, amazing things happen!* First, you begin to feel better because you have alerted your mind powers to the possibility of good. Your mind and body then unconsciously start to expect something good to happen.

As you continue to develop spiritual and mental strength by pronouncing negative situations good, you begin to feel freer of fear, because you have begun to unload the burden of negative words, thoughts, and feelings with which you have been unconsciously struggling, and which have lodged themselves in the small of the back.

As you persist in your decrees and expectancies of good you open the way mentally and physically for startling changes to take place in your body and affairs. *You can confidently expect good things to happen when you take your stand and pronounce everything good.* Since good is another name for strength, you release omnipotent strength into every phase of your world.[5]

This principle of good, as a form of strength, applies no matter what the situation is:

If it is your body that needs a blessing, do not call it old, weak, sick, or tired. Declare instead: "I PRONOUNCE EVERY ATOM AND CELL OF MY BODY GOOD, LIFE-FILLED."

If it is your pocketbook, bank account, or financial affairs that are troubling you, do not refer to them as empty, lacking, or exhausted. Instead affirm: "I PRONOUNCE YOU GOOD, FILLED TO OVERFLOWING WITH ABUNDANT IDEAS AND ABUNDANT SUPPLY NOW."

If it is a relative, neighbor, or business associate that is burdening you, do not refer to him as nosy, stingy, cruel, careless or selfish. Declare: "I PRONOUNCE YOU GOOD, CREATED IN THE IMAGE OF GOD'S GOOD, FILLED WITH DIVINE LOVE AND WISDOM."

If it is your work that burdens you, do not label it as dull, uninteresting, tiresome. Declare: "I PRONOUNCE YOU GOOD, IMPORTANT, WELL-PAYING, OF BENEFIT TO GOD AND MAN."

If it is your family that burdens you, no longer decree that they are uncooperative, unappreciative, unkind, demanding. Instead decree: "I PRONOUNCE MY FAMILY AND ALL OUR RELATIONSHIPS GOOD."

---

5. See the chapter, "Your Gateway to Successful Living" in *The Prosperity Secrets of the Ages.*

If it is the negative thoughts of your mind that bother you, such as depression, discouragement, a troublesome, burdened feeling that you are trying to cast off, declare: "I PRONOUNCE YOU GOOD, ILLUMINED, INSPIRED, UPLIFTED BY DIVINE WISDOM."

As you begin each day, invoke your spiritual, mental, and physical strength by declaring:"I PRONOUNCE THIS DAY AND ALL ITS ACTIVITES GOOD." At the end of the day, garner the blessings from it by declaring: "IT WAS A GOOD DAY. BEHOLD, IT WAS VERY GOOD."

It is easier to make these decrees for the various departments of your life when you realize that you live in a friendly, responsive universe that is eager to show forth its true nature of good in your life.

Be steadfast, strong, and steady to the thought of good in your world, and you will, thereby, establish strength in mind and body. Indeed, your health is receptive and responsive to your decrees of good, which release deeper levels of energy within your mind power of strength, located in the small of the back, and which flow from it out into your entire body.

You can deliberately activate the strength center in the back by relaxing and "calling" it into activity for you. "STRENGTH, STRENGTH, STRENGTH. I AM A TOWER OF STRENGTH WITHIN AND WITHOUT. I LET ALL BURDENS FALL FROM MY SHOULDERS. I LET ANXIETY DROP FROM MY MIND. I LET ALL FEAR SLIP AWAY FROM MY HEART. I LET ALL OUTER AFFAIRS BE RELEASED. I LET EVERY SHACKLE BE LOOSENED. DIVINE STRENGTH IS MAKING WISE AND TRUE ADJUSTMENT IN EVERY PHASE OF MY LIFE. I RELAX, REJOICE, AND LET IT."

Your healing power of

JUDGMENT

— 4 —

A woman who had stomach trouble often said in self-pity, "Doctors just cannot build me up. My food does not digest properly. I have to almost starve myself to death in order to survive."

As a nutritionist, she made it a point to eat the proper foods and could not understand why she had health problems. She refused to believe that her health problems were based on her unhealthy emotions and not on her healthy diet.

Her favorite pastime was finding fault with her husband. This gave her a certain neurotic pleasure which she did not wish to give up. She preferred to continue to condemn, find fault with, and dictate to her husband — which meant keeping her stomach trouble — rather than to emotionally free him, thereby, finding freedom from her own health problems. She was her own worst enemy and was painfully "enjoying" every minute of it!

There is an old saying, "You cannot let your thoughts

dwell upon your neighbor's faults without harm to yourself." This woman proved it.

People who criticize their loved ones should be reminded of that old Spanish proverb: "He who does not laugh at the faults of his loved ones does not love at all."

STOMACH IS THE JUDGMENT CENTER

Your mind power of judgment is located at the pit of the stomach in the center of the solar plexus region of the body as shown in Figure 4-1. Wrong use of the judg-

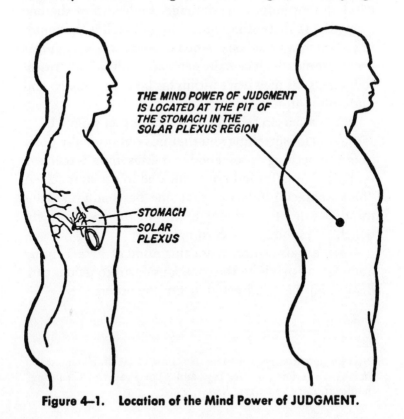

THE MIND POWER OF JUDGMENT IS LOCATED AT THE PIT OF THE STOMACH IN THE SOLAR PLEXUS REGION

STOMACH
SOLAR PLEXUS

Figure 4–1.   Location of the Mind Power of JUDGMENT.

ment power causes all kinds of stomach trouble, as well as related ills of the entire abdominal region.

People who say that certain foods do not agree with them are often people like this woman. *They use their judgment faculty wrongly* by complaining about and finding fault with other people. It isn't their food that does not agree with them, so much as it is their own disagreeable attitudes. People with stomach trouble are usually "quiet complainers" that you will cross the street in the middle of a block to avoid!

The words "condemn" and "damn" come from the same root word, meaning to "damage." Strong, condemning judgments damage the health of the one doing the fault-finding. Since the stomach is the center of judgment in the body, when a person strongly judges other people, he personally gets the results of his critical judgments, as they react within his body as stomach and abdominal upsets.

When a person tells you he has an upset stomach, he is unconsciously telling you that he is emotionally upset about something or somebody, and his upset is reacting on his judgment mind power located in the stomach. A "bad stomach" indicates that one has badly used his mind power of judgment at the pit of the stomach, which is responding accordingly.

One can also suffer from this ailment by accepting and soaking up either the conscious or subconscious condemnation being directed at him by others.[1]

---

1. To remedy this, see "The 'No' Law of Healing" chapter in *The Dynamic Laws of Healing,* and "The Prayer of Cleansing" chapter in *Pray and Grow Rich.*

BELIEF IN INJUSTICE CAUSES STOMACH TROUBLE

Often the mind power of judgment is misused as a feeling of injustice, fault-finding, and condemnation. People who have a martyr complex and feel that they have suffered injustice through circumstances and because of other people, usually have stomach trouble.

Timid people who feel that life is unfair to them and who feel that they are being "elbowed" out of their just rewards by more aggressive people, often have stomach trouble. Many unhappy, seemingly unaccountable experiences that come in life are simply the result of secret feelings of injustice.[2]

A woman recently wrote: "I cannot understand why I have never been able to get a healing from a severe stomach and abdominal ailment which has plagued me for years. I have suffered so much recently that I have been confined to my bed."

Then she revealingly wrote: "My family and friends tell me I should sue my doctors because they have not healed me of this dreadful stomach trouble. I have spent hundreds of dollars with them and am as sick as ever. Should I sue my doctors for not healing me?"

How foolish of her. Of course not!

The only person she should have considered suing was herself and her own fault-finding attitudes! This woman had not yet learned the first law of healing: "As he thinketh within himself, so is he" (Proverbs 23:7), which might be paraphrased as a health proverb: "As *he thinketh within his mind, so is his body—especially his stomach!*"

---

2. See the chapter, "How to Overcome Injustice" in *The Prosperity Secrets of the Ages*.

This woman had a feeling of injustice which she had been "nursing" and keeping alive for years. As she had misused her judgment mind power, located at the pit of the stomach, it had naturally responded in a similar way, producing ill health in that very area.

She was quickly advised that her doctors would never be able to heal her body until she cooperated by healing her mind of unjust accusations toward them. For this purpose it was suggested that she affirm daily: "I USE MY JUDGMENT POWERS RIGHTLY. THE DIVINE LAW OF JUSTICE IS NOW WORKING PERFECTLY THROUGH ME TOWARD ALL PEOPLE, AND THROUGH ALL PEOPLE TOWARD ME. I DO NOT JUDGE OTHERS AS REGARDS THEIR GUILT OR INNOCENCE. I CAST EVERY JUDGMENT ON THE CHRIST WITHIN AND I GO FREE TO NEW LIFE, HEALTH, STRENGTH, AND TO NEW PEACE OF MIND. ALL THINGS ARE WORKING TOGETHER FOR MY GOOD, AND I AM WORKING WITH THEM IN A SPIRIT OF LOVE AND JUSTICE."

This woman needed to realize that things don't "just happen," but that *things happen justly*.

The prevailing tendency of judgment is to express caution, fearfulness, complaints, and condemnation, which always reacts upon the one doing the fault-finding. Jesus gave a healing treatment for this when He said, "Neither do I condemn thee; go thy way; from henceforth sin no more." (John 8:11) "He that is without sin among you, let him first cast a stone."(John:8:7)

We can establish order, justice and prosperity in our personal affairs by invoking directly the divine law of justice. Instead of fighting for our rights, we may obtain them by mentally declaring: "I ASK NOTHING IN SELFISHNESS, AND MY OWN COMES TO ME THROUGH DIVINE LAW."

Also, we must be willing for the principle of justice to work both ways. Not only should we desire to receive justice ourselves, but we must be willing to grant it to others. Forgiveness and mercy are included in the concept of divine justice. If we desire forgiveness and justice, we must first grant them to others.[3]

KEEN INTELLIGENCE IN STOMACH REGION

It is usually a surprise to learn that this mind power of judgment, which includes discrimination, wisdom, and all departments of the mind pertaining to "knowing," is found in the pit of the stomach. We usually think of good judgment as a mind power which we assume functions from the brain located in the cranium.

However, it is quite logical that the judgment mind power would be located in the stomach, because that is the function of the stomach—to judge, to digest.

The stomach acts as a sentinel of the body, challenging everything that is sent to it. It registers our most delicate and secret emotions. The attitudes of people who assume too much responsibility, and are concerned about matters that are none of their business, affect the whole digestive process from the alimentary canal, through the stomach, liver, spleen, kidneys, right into the intestines.

Just how strongly our emotions affect the stomach area is shown by the fact that the solar plexus region, in which the stomach is located, is the most important of the centers of the sympathetic system. The solar plexus nerve center functions as a mirror. Upon its sensitive nerve centers are reflected man's deep feelings; all strong

---

3. See the chapter, "The Surprise Law of Healing" in *The Dynamic Laws of Healing*.

thought impulses thrown upon the solar plexus are sent through the nerves to all parts of the body.

All emotional imbalance is felt in the solar plexus region. Fear and excitement cause nausea and excessive emotional activity in this region. A sinking, sickening feeling at the pit of the stomach quickly develops when we condemn ourselves or others, or feel we have been unjustly treated. Through emotional imbalance in the solar plexus region, negative psychic phenomena are sometimes produced. This explains why emotionally unbalanced people have psychotic obsessions.

Doctors have long known that the solar plexus is filled with a keen intelligence. Because of this they have called the solar plexus the great "body brain." In it is found grey matter similar to that in the brain.

The very keen intelligence of the solar plexus nerve center reacts instantly to every pleasure, as well as to every sorrow—both of which register at the pit of the stomach. You have had sudden shock hit you at the pit of the stomach. Hate, passion, fear and kindred emotions all strike there and affect the action of the inter-connected vital organs.

Through this large nerve center, your stomach is closely associated with your heart, as well as with the mind powers located in the head. *No organ of your body is more quickly affected by your moods than your stomach!* This explains why sulking, moody people often have stomach trouble.

Every bit of food that you take into your stomach must be chemically treated at this mind center in the stomach before it can be distributed to the many parts of the body. In fact, the body awaits the stomach's wise judgment to supply it with the proper materials to build bones, muscles, nerves, and every part of the organism.

When we study the body and its many functions, we see how much depends upon the intelligent ability of our judgment power as it functions through the stomach. It is also easy to see how misuse of one's judgment power plays havoc on one's health. This explains why critical people become sick people, as well as why sick people have been critical!

STOMACH AS THE SEAT OF MEMORY

The power by which you are justified or condemned is within you. You can be sure that all injustice that has come to you sprang up from a seed of your own planting! All that has come to you of good or ill was first set into motion by your own good or ill thoughts and actions. To clear away unjust thoughts and results, affirm: "I NOW FORGIVE ALL APPARENT INJUSTICE. I FORGIVE MYSELF FOR HAVING FIRST SET IT IN MOTION. DIVINE JUSTICE NOW MOLDS MY PRESENT AND FUTURE PERFECTLY. GOD'S GOODNESS WITHIN ME AND AROUND ME IS NOW RELEASED. I NOW FULFILL MY PERFECT DESTINY."

The fact that the judgment mind power is located at the pit of the stomach at the solar plexus nerve center gives us another clue to much illness. This abdominal region is the seat of the subconscious mind. You know people who have stomach trouble, who seem very nice, and you protest, "But they do not condemn or find fault. They are not filled with envy, jealousy or spite."

Often it is not one's immediate conscious thoughts that cause stomach trouble. It may be the negative memories of the past of bitter, hard, unjust experiences, that are stored in the subconscious memory nature located in the stomach that now cause health problems there. *The stomach is filled with memory cells which go on quietly functioning subconsciously long after you've forgotten about them.*[4]

A professional man suffered from acute indigestion and liver trouble. To his friends and clients, he seemed a casual, bland, pleasant man. But this man was in the midst of a bitter divorce action involving his wife of many years. His close relatives realized how much he hated her, never speaking of her except in the most bitter terms.

His stomach and liver trouble had begun when his marital problems had begun. This man had quietly stored up feelings of hate, fear, injustice and bitterness about his wife for a number of years. When the court battle reached the boiling point, so did all his old emotions—which boiled up out of his memory which nature had located in the cells of the stomach. Indigestion and, later, ulcers developed.

INDIGESTION AND ALCOHOLISM HEALED

Malice is an acid state of mind which expresses as spite, the desire to get even, the intention to hurt others. These strong feelings release extra acidity into the blood from the various organs, causing ulcers, cancers, and all types of destruction. The stomach, as well as the heart, is especially affected by malice and jealousy. *You need not be jealous of, nor judge another, for you can be sure that person will be judged by the health problems that his own thoughts and actions will produce in his mind and body!*

---

4. See the chapter, "The Secret of Overcoming Hard Conditions" in *The Prosperity Secrets of the Ages.*

In order to be healthy, both physically and emotionally, one must get free of condemnation and unforgiveness. *Hatred and unforgiveness cause a hardness and rigidity in the cells of the stomach which particularly affect one's health there.*

A housewife had suffered from chronic indigestion for 12 years and had sought help everywhere. Previous medical help no longer availed, since she could no longer digest even her medicine! In despair this woman finally visited a spiritual counselor in search of healing.

Her indigestion had begun after her husband started drinking 12 years previously. As his drinking had increased, so had her indigestion. The more he drank, the more cruel he became, and the more his wife and children feared him, their fear finally turning to hate.

The counselor told his wife she could begin healing her stomach trouble by forgiving her husband. She was asked to daily affirm: "I FULLY AND FREELY FORGIVE YOU. I LOOSE YOU AND LET YOU GO. I LET GO AND LET GOD."

The wife decided she could more easily do this if she could be away from her husband for a few weeks; so she bravely told him she was taking their children for a visit to her mother. Ordinarily he would not have permitted it, but the affirmations of forgiveness and release seemed to be working, and he did not protest. While away she daily affirmed forgiveness and release, adding: "NEITHER DO I CONDEMN THEE. BE THOU MADE WHOLE."

Upon her return her husband said, "Something came over me while you were away, something I cannot explain. But I know I will never drink again. When I think of my previous drinking, it disgusts me. It is all over. I feel both you and God have forgiven me." With this realization, both his drinking and her indigestion disappeared.

STOMACH TROUBLE HEALED

Indigestion is the result of what has been taken in by the mind without liking or approving of it. Indigestion, ulcers, even cancer of the stomach, result from feeding on negative thoughts, words and feelings which do not agree with the body. The judgment center at the pit of the stomach reacts to these undesirable emotions by trying to throw them off; then the discomfort of indigestion ensues.

A housewife suffered from indigestion so severe that she could hardly bear it. When the mental cause was uncovered, it was revealed she had a terrible fear lest her husband lose his job. Since there were complex human relations problems involved, a great anxiety had gripped her that he would be unjustly treated.

The counselor gave this affirmation, which both this woman and her husband began using together daily: "GOD IS ADJUSTING EVERYTHING IN THIS SITUATION NOW. THE PLACE THAT GOD HAS FOR US TO FILL QUICKLY MANIFESTS."

First, all fear and worry left her mind, and within a few weeks the complex situation had adjusted itself. Two employees who had been unjustly fired were asked to return to the company. This woman's husband was advanced in salary and also given a promotion. Her stomach trouble quickly responded to release from fear, worry, and previous beliefs in injustice, as the indigestion faded away.

Sensitiveness to bad news, secret fears and worries, unkind thoughts and words, as well as general inharmony in one's life, cause indigestion. *Affirming that all things work together for good causes the stomach to again work in a normal way.*

If all the time and money that are spent to regulate one's diet were spent to regulate one's thoughts and purify one's emotions, diseases of the stomach would totally disappear!

A "BORN WORRIER" HEALED

A businessman was a "born worrier." Everything preyed upon his mind and as a result, he suffered from chronic indigestion and other stomach trouble. A spiritual counselor advised him to relax daily and release both his business and family affairs, as well as all his possessions, to his Creator: "FATHER, THESE ARE ALL YOURS. YOU CARE FOR THEM. I RELAX AND LET GO, KNOWING THAT YOU ARE CARRYING THE RESPONSIBILITY."

Through the daily practice of relaxation and release, this man's stomach trouble diminished. Finally he reported that he could eat anything he wanted again and that he no longer worried because he now knew that all things were working together for good, and not for evil.

For the stomach affirm often: "I AGREE WITH WHAT I EAT, AND WHAT I EAT AGREES WITH ME. I AM AT PEACE WITH ALL PEOPLE AND ALL SITUATIONS NOW. I DO NOT RESIST OR ANTAGONIZE ANYTHING OR ANYBODY. MY STOMACH IS STRONG, WISE, AND ENERGETIC. I ALWAYS THINK AND SPEAK OF IT AS CAPABLE OF DOING ITS WORK PERFECTLY. I DO NOT IMPOSE ON MY STOMACH BY OVERLOADING IT. I AM GUIDED BY DIVINE WISDOM IN MY EATING AND DRINKING, AND I FOLLOW ITS GUIDANCE. I AM NO LONGER ANXIOUS ABOUT WHAT I EAT OR DRINK. AFTER EATING, I QUIETLY RELAX, RELEASE ALL CARES, AND GIVE MY STOMACH AN OPPORTUNITY TO DO ITS PERFECT WORK."

MENTAL CAUSES OF DIABETES

The pancreas gland, located in the solar plexus region as shown in Figure 4-2, is concerned with the mobilization of energy for both physical and mental purposes. Its secretions are vital not only to the digestive processes, but also to the metabolism of sugar which the cells, muscles, and nerves require for their existence.

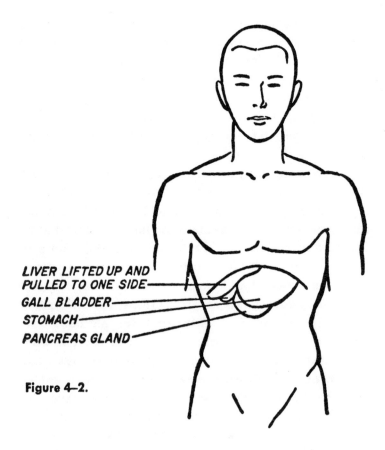

LIVER LIFTED UP AND
PULLED TO ONE SIDE
GALL BLADDER
STOMACH
PANCREAS GLAND

Figure 4–2.

Location of the Pancreas in the Solar Plexus Region.

Diabetes results when the pancreas gland is not functioning properly. The body is then unable to utilize sugar which is excreted into the urine. Continuous grief or emotional shocks cause diabetes; also severe judgment of one's self or others. The mind must be purged of condemnation, which affects the pancreas gland located just below the stomach, before permanent healing is possible.

A lawyer discovered in a strange way that he had what was considered an incurable case of diabetes. He had a thorough physical examination for the purpose of obtaining life insurance, but was told by the examining physician that he had only six months to live.

Within the next three months he lost 60 pounds worrying about the death sentence hanging over him. One day while riding a train to a distant town for an appointment with a client, he began chatting with a fellow passenger and spoke of his incurable condition.

To his astonishment, the stranger calmly informed him that he, himself, had been healed of the same disease, and handed him a piece of inspirational literature to read on healing. In it he found these words: *"Release all condemnation of yourself and others and daily declare, 'Only the good is true!' "*

Daily this attorney began affirming, "I NO LONGER CONDEMN MYSELF OR OTHERS. NEITHER DO I CONDEMN MY HEALTH. ONLY THE GOOD IS TRUE." From that time forward, he began to feel better in mind and body. A little later he was so confident of a complete healing, that he dispensed with all medication.

Three months later, at the time predicted for him to die, he again visited the examining physician and was pronounced completely healed. A decade later, at the time this man related his story, he had had no further health problems.

KIDNEYS, LIVER, SPLEEN ADVERSELY
AFFECTED BY FALSE JUDGMENTS

False judgments are always reflected in the stomach as well as in the organs of elimination. When the kidneys become inflamed through over-judgment, the liver is also sympathetically disturbed.

The liver is a large gland situated in the right and upper part of the abdomen, which collects the blood from the abdominal organs and produces bile. It also assimilates and stores sugar among other things for the needs of the body. The liver's important function is purifying the fluids of the body.

It is affected by man's judging or his critical thoughts, and one of its functions is to cast out those thoughts which are useless. *Fixed regrets may produce dangerous diseases of the liver.* Supposedly incurable diseases of the liver come from looking back and thinking of one's mistakes as incurable, unforgivable, and from judging one's self unmercifully.

Your general attitudes toward life are also registered at the liver. A continual sense of injustice, a feeling of bitterness, a belief that things are going wrong and you do not know how to right them are feelings that can result in a diseased condition of the liver.

When you forgive yourself and others, and free your mind from misjudgment, bitterness, injustice, intolerance and revenge, the stomach, liver and every organ of the body benefits. Declare often for this purpose: "ALL BITTERNESS AND BELIEF IN INJUSTICE NOW PASS FROM MY MIND AND BODY. DIVINE JUSTICE, DIVINE ADJUSTMENT NOW APPEAR."

DISTRESS OF MIND SLOWS DOWN
THE LIVER FUNCTIONS

Looking back continually in self-condemnation and regret can even lead to death. Resentment and pettiness are also reflected adversely in the liver. Tolerance of one's self, compassion for others, less judgment and more harmony with others, bring a warm glow and increased circulation to the liver, resulting in improved health in other parts of the body, too. For this purpose affirm: "I AM NOT MISJUDGED NOR DO I MISJUDGE OTHERS. I DO NOT CRITICIZE OR CONDEMN. I HOLD NO BITTER, REVENGEFUL THOUGHTS TOWARD OTHERS. I DO NOT BELIEVE I HAVE BEEN OR WILL BE UNJUSTLY TREATED. I RELEASE ALL JUDGMENT TO THE DIVINE LAW OF JUSTICE. I AM AT PEACE WITH GOD AND MAN."

IMPORTANCE OF HEALING THE SPLEEN

The spleen is a large glandlike organ near the end of the stomach. The ancients felt that the spleen was the seat of anger, agitation, and melancholy in the body. The spleen is a distributor of energy and any mental commotion affects it adversely. Rheumatism, arthritis, neuralgia, inflammation, ulcers, hemorrhaging, and displacement of organs often result from the anger and agitation released in and through the spleen to other parts of the body. For healing of the spleen affirm: "I NO LONGER ACCUSE MYSELF OR OTHERS OF EVIL. FORGIVING, I AM FORGIVEN AND HEALED."

While ulcers and cancers usually affect women in the breast or genital organs, in men they usually appear in the stomach, mouth, or alimentary canal. *Anger especially weakens the judgment mind power in the stomach. Extreme emotional conflicts send the cells on a rampage, breaking down the cell structure and eating up the flesh.*

An incurable disease can be traced to incurable condemnation of one's self or others. Cancer originates in all kinds of malice, such as hatred, revenge, jealousy, the desire to undermine another, animosity, envy, deep resentment, malicious gossip, anger, vicious opposition, which often express themselves through a critical, backbiting disposition.

Since the stomach (judgment center) and the heart (love center) are both located in the central part of the body, this indicates that love and judgment must work together to balance each other. When they do, a fault-finding disposition can be overcome, and both stomach and heart respond with improved health. The close physical connection between the stomach and heart are metaphysically symbolized in the fact that the disciples James and John were brothers. James symbolizes judgment and John symbolizes love.

Use of the following statements daily will improve one's health in both the stomach and abdominal areas:

"ALL IDEAS OF JUDGMENT, REVENGE, PUNISHMENT, AND EVIL ARE ELIMINATED FROM MY MIND AND BODY NOW. INSTEAD I BEHOLD THE LOVE, MERCY, AND GOODNESS OF GOD AT WORK IN MY MIND, BODY, AFFAIRS, AND RELATIONSHIPS WITH ALL MANKIND.

"I LET ALL PEOPLE BE HAPPY! I LET ALL PEOPLE BE PROSPEROUS! I LET ALL PEOPLE BE FREE! IN SO DOING, MY OWN HAPPINESS, PROSPERITY, AND FREEDOM ARE ASSURED.

"THERE IS NO CONDEMNATION IN ME, FOR ME OR AGAINST ME. PRIDE, RESENTMENT, AND JEALOUSY HAVE NO POWER OVER ME. I DO NOT ACCUSE MYSELF OR OTHERS OF GUILT.

NO THOUGHT OF SELFISHNESS CAN POSSESS ME. ALL THE
GOODNESS OF GOD IS NOW MINE TO USE AND ENJOY. MY
MIND, BODY, AFFAIRS, AND RELATIONSHIPS ARE NOW
CHARGED WITH JOY AND FREEDOM. I REJOICE IN MY MEN-
TAL AND PHYSICAL PERFECTION NOW. ALL THE GOOD MY
HEART DESIRES IS COMING TO ME NOW!"

THE STOMACH IS THE CENTER OF
PHYSICAL AND MENTAL SUBSTANCE

Just as the stomach is the physical center of substance
in the body, receiving one's food, digesting it, and sending it on as nourishment to all parts of the body, it is also
the mental center of substance in the body.

The substance center of the body is affected by the
idea of substance held in mind. Many a businessman suffering from financial problems also suffers from stomach
trouble. Lack of sufficient prosperity in one's life which
produces financial problems, reacts upon the substance
center in the stomach and causes numerous health problems there.

Also the habit of condemning persons who seem to enjoy undeserved success causes a negative reaction upon
one's own substance center in the stomach and, conse-
quently, upon one's own financial affairs. There is a
story in my book *The Dynamic Laws of Prosperity* of
how a man wrecked his own health by condemning other
people's success and then regained it when he regained
the right mental perspective.

Whereas too much weight often results from trying to
accumulate too many possessions or by holding to
unpleasant memories that should be forgotten, worry,
fear, nagging and destructive thoughts and words wear

the body down to abnormal thinness. Too much zeal
and ambition burn up the energy of the body faster than
it is generated, whereas, drastic economy robs both mind
and body of needed substance. This leads to a nervous,
crabbed, gloomy, distrustful, discontented outlook, sap-
ping both mind and body, and especially affecting the
substance center in the stomach.

When you turn your attention to the substance center
in the stomach and meditate often upon "Divine
substance," you purify negative emotions stored there.
You also release new energy, life, and substance into the
functions of the stomach, liver, heart, out into the entire abdominal region, and finally into the whole body.
Renewed energy, improved health, and peace of mind
follow.

HOW TO PRODUCE HEALINGS IN THE STOMACH

Since the substance center is physically located at the
nerve center back of the stomach, the loves and hates of
the mind are precipitated to this ganglionic receptacle
of thought and become crystallized there. *What we love
and what we hate build cells of joy or of pain in the
stomach.*

When the mind has been lashed by emotional torrents
of ill thoughts and words, the cells of the whole organism
are shattered and exhaustion and depression follow.
Nervous prostration, which readily affects the stomach
and its digestive process, is the first result of exhausted
nerve force.

A restful state of mind is a healing state of mind.
Steadfast affirmations of peace will harmonize the whole
body structure and open the way to healthy conditions:

"I AM AT PEACE BECAUSE I TRUST DIVINE JUSTICE TO REGULATE ALL MY AFFAIRS NOW. I HAVE FAITH IN DIVINE JUSTICE AND I NOW TRUST IT TO SET RIGHT EVERY CONDITION OF MY LIFE."

Many persons doubt that there is an infinite law of justice working in all things. Let them now take heart and know that this law has not worked in their affairs previously because they have not "called" it into activity. When we call our inner forces into action, the universal law begins its great work in us, and all the laws both great and small fall into line and work for us. One lady was healed of cancer of the stomach by affirming: "FROM THIS TIME FORWARD, I WILL PUT DOUBTS, CRITICISMS, AND QUIBBLINGS ASIDE."

The law of justice can be established by the use of definite affirmations, and the results make it worth it! When a person uses his judgment rightly in dealing with others, he becomes more loving, refrains from all manner of criticism, and keeps his eye single to the good. The mind thinks more clearly. The expressions of love and affection are more spontaneous. A more kindly disposition will be in evidence and a renewal of the whole man takes place.

In your quiet, meditative periods, relax and fix your attention gently at the pit of the stomach, affirming: "DIVINE JUSTICE IS NOW ESTABLISHED IN ME."

Then—dwell upon the healing idea of "DIVINE SUBSTANCE."

"I AM SATISFIED WITH DIVINE SUBSTANCE. THE SUBSTANCE OF GOD NOW ERASES ALL FATIGUE FROM MY BODY, RENEWS TISSUES, AND REPLENISHES ENERGY. DIVINE SUBSTANCE STABILIZES MY MIND AND PROSPERS MY AFFAIRS. EVERY LONGING OF MY SOUL AND EVERY NEED OF MY LIFE IS NOW FULFILLED. I AM SATISFIED WITH DIVINE SUBSTANCE."

As you awaken the judgment-substance center in the stomach area, you may find several things happening. Your taste in foods may change, becoming more refined. You may have a strange taste in your mouth, as old bitterness is released from the judgment center, and then an intense thirst may be felt. Your solar plexus area may seem more expanded; then it may decrease, becoming more relaxed. It is all an indication that an expansion of your judgment mind power is taking place. In any event, continue your mental work and let the healing results be what they may.

Your healing power of

LOVE

— 5 —

Love has been described as the physician of the universe; as the medicine that heals all disease. Love can heal all ills because love is more than an emotion or even a spiritual quality. Love is also a mind power.

This mind power of love is located in the region of the heart, which is the center of love in the body. Any time a person violates the law of love through expressing hate, fear, resentment, and other unhealthy emotions, it affects his heart, and often the lungs, chest and breast area too. *When a person has heart trouble or cancer of the lungs or breast, a deliberate release of the mind power of love from within himself can help clear his mind and body of this undesirable condition.*

HOW LOVE HEALED HEART PAINS

A woman who had had a continuous pain in her heart for more than a year learned of the mind power of love located at the heart, and she began saying to her heart daily: "MY HEART IS CONTROLLED BY DIVINE LOVE. IT IS NOW CLEANSED OF ALL MISUNDERSTANDING, BITTERNESS, DOUBT, DEPRESSION, DISHARMONY OR DISEASE. IT IS FREE AND UNBURDENED. MY HEART IS UNTROUBLED AND UNAFRAID."

She told her heart that it now expressed perfectly just as it had in her youth, and she dwelled upon healing promises from the Bible, such as "Let not your heart be troubled, neither let it be fearful." (John 14:27) "Keep thy heart with all diligence, for out of it are the issues of life." (Proverbs 4:23) Her heart trouble diminished as she activated her mind power of love, which made her magnetic to her heart's desires. A former heartache turned to heart-felt blessings in mind, body, and affairs.

ONE PERSON'S RECOGNITION OF LOVE HELPS HEAL ANOTHER'S HEART CONDITION

Someone else recognizing and calling forth the mind power of love can help a person activate his healing power, as evidenced by the following inspiring account of a dramatic true experience:

"A patient had been brought into the hospital where I worked, following a severe heart attack. His doctor held little hope for his recovery. I remained with him while a private nurse was being contacted. Suddenly he stopped breathing, his blood pressure dropped, and there was no heartbeat. While his doctor was on his way to the room, I called the patient's name, loudly affirming to him over and over: 'YOUR HEART IS RIGHT WITH GOD. DIVINE LOVE IS HEALING YOU NOW.'

"I continued decreeing this affirmation while setting up the emergency equipment. After the doctor administered an injection into the heart, the patient began to respond, though by all medical standards he had no chance of recovery. Nevertheless, he continued to improve and later was able to go home, though his doctor warned him he would never be able to work again. He told the doctor he believed he had been healed of this long-standing heart condition by something the nurse had said to him when he was almost gone.

"I gave him the affirmation I had used for his recovery and he continued affirming, 'MY HEART IS RIGHT WITH GOD. DIVINE LOVE HAS HEALED ME NOW.' In three months he was back on his job feeling better than he had in years. His problems with his family, which had upset him and had caused his previous heart condition, were soon healed, too.

"For the first time in years he not only had good health, but also a happy home life. He was truly a changed man. When I last saw him, four years later, he had had no more attacks although he worked hard every day and at a job he had been told he would never be able to do again! He spent his leisure hours working in his garden."

HOW TO DEVELOP LOVE

It has been estimated that 70 percent of all disease is caused by suppressed emotion. Regret, sorrow, and remorse tear down the cells of the body. Thoughts of hate generate a deadly poison in the body, which can kill if not neutralized by love. All disease comes from violation of the law of love. Resentment and anger act as boomerangs producing sickness and sorrow.

Love is an awakener. Psychologists have found that people who know how to express love are healthier; they tend to get sick less and to recover more quickly. They age more slowly, and have better color, clearer skins, better posture and circulation than do the depressed, cynical, bitter types of people.

Thoughts of love cause a beneficial chemical change to take place in the body. Thoughts of love bring forth life, renew health, and even change thoughts of death to thoughts of life. *Just as the heart equalizes the life flow in the body, so love harmonizes the thoughts of the mind, bringing peace to both mind and body.* You connect your soul-forces with whatever you center your love upon.

You should make it a practice to meditate daily on the mind power of love. You can call it alive within you by centering your attention on the love center at the heart and affirming: "DIVINE LOVE, MANIFEST THYSELF IN ME NOW." As you think about love with your attention at the heart, a quickening will follow. *Mental concentration upon love will produce a positive love current, which goes forth to break up and dissolve opposing thoughts of hate. The thought of hate will be dissolved not only in the mind of the thinker, but also in the minds of those with whom he comes in contact or thinks about.*

A doctor's wife began establishing harmony with someone who had been very difficult after affirming for the person: "I LOVE YOU AND YOU LOVE ME." Opposition disappeared between them. A housewife's formula for getting along with troublesome people is to mentally say to them: "I LOVE YOU, I BLESS YOU, I HAVE FAITH IN YOU."

A woman who knew of the healing force of love was waylaid by a tramp. She looked him steadily in the eye and said, "God loves you." He released his hold on her and slunk away. Another woman saw a man beating a horse that could not pull a load up a hill. She silently said to the man. "THE LOVE OF GOD FILLS YOUR HEART AND YOU ARE TENDER AND KIND." He unhitched the horse, and the grateful animal walked directly over to the house where the woman was and put his nose against the window behind which she stood.

WILLFULNESS CAUSES HEART TROUBLE

The love current is not a projection of the will. It is simply a setting free of a natural, equalizing, harmonizing force which has been dammed up and unused.

Most people think that when they love a person, they have a right to dominate and rule that person's life. *When people try to rule and dominate others, calling it "love," they often have heart trouble!*

This happens because a dominating and possessive will affects the heart, which cannot stand to be pressured. The will is the lifeline of man. The mind power of will is supposed to work through understanding, as explained later in Chapter 9. But usually the will tries to have its own way without the help of understanding. As it attempts to force its will upon others, the heart is affected.

We often see the damaging results of domination in the parent-child relationship. The old idea was that a woman who did not worry about her children was not a good mother. Now psychologists state that mothers' fear and domination are responsible for many of the diseases and accidents which come into the lives of children.

When parents fear for their children and are anxious about them, that anxiety is transferred to the children. A feeling of limitation, suppression, inharmony follows, which produces behavior and health problems in both children and parents.

Parents can actually smother their children so much with what they think is love, that they literally drive the child's soul right out of the body, and death follows.

This happens often in adults, too, where there is strong possessiveness. Often the one being possessed either develops heart trouble and is chronically sick, or else leaves this earth plane completely. Then the one left often cannot understand why, thinking they have given all of their "love."

Many adults, as a result of being forced, possessed, smothered in childhood, have hard unyielding places in the subconscious mind that do not yield easily to the spoken word of truth. Persistent affirmations of Divine love break up these hard places in the subconscious and the diseased thought patterns gathered there.

Love does not possess or dominate, and is not willful. Love is a harmonizing, balancing, freeing quality of mind and body. True love does harmonize, balance, and free rather than bind.

Heart trouble in both adults and children is often due to the feeling of being smothered by the demanding love and affection of another person, especially when that possessiveness is bearing down upon a sensitive mind. This binding kind of love squeezes and stifles the freedom of a person, as it causes both heart and lung diseases—sometimes in the possessive one, but more often in the one being possessed.

One woman's possessiveness was reflected in her whole family: Her husband suffered from heart trouble and chronic business failure. Her daughter suffered from colds, bouts with pneumonia, and was especially susceptible to lung disturbances. Her son suffered from asthma—long known as a "suppression disease." The Biblical admonition of Jesus: "A man's foes shall be they of his own household" (Matthew 10:36) surely applied to this family.

Sadly enough, this wife and mother busied herself dominating and "sacrificing" for her family, none of whom were healthy, happy or successful, while neglecting the development of her own soul qualities. She had not yet learned that the surest way of helping others is to first improve one's own consciousness.

The notion of self-sacrifice as an element of love is false and leads only to the weakening of the character of the person for whom the sacrificing is made. The "self-sacrificer" frequently interferes seriously with the individual development of another, as well as hampering his own soul's growth. This well-meaning but misguided woman proved this. The home, which should be most beneficial to our health and happiness, is often most dangerous and destructive to both our mental and physical health.

LOVE CAN EVEN HEAL FALLING HAIR

Many ills are caused by unpleasantness from the past which are stored in the subconscious mind. A lovely young girl was losing her hair. It was falling out in bunches, leaving bald spots all over her head. Medical treatment for her condition included shots that were being administered right into the head area. But nothing seemed to help.

This young lady was desperate because she was planning to be married shortly and feared being bald on her wedding day! A short chat quickly revealed the emotional problem causing this loss. Her parents had tried to force her into high scholastic and social achievements in college, and she had disappointed them by flunking out on both counts. Condemnation and tension between them had resulted. The feeling of having lost her parents' love and respect was reflected subconsciously through loss of hair.

When this was pointed out to both the daughter and parents, and reassurance of their love was expressed, the feeling of restoration was reflected as her hair began to grow again.

HOW TO GAIN FREEDOM WITH LOVE

The heart is a pump. It circulates blood through several large valves. If anything constricts or limits the flow of blood through these valves, then there is heart trouble. A feeling of being possessed, held down, or forced, causes a sense of limitation around the heart that acts as a vise, constricting the activity of the valves. Heart trouble results.

There has to be a sense of freedom in connection with love at its heart center, or it will "act up" trying to get its freedom. You ask, "But how can one clear up a possessive, binding love that causes heart trouble and lung diseases?"[1]

In healing the victim of a possessive love, it is good to affirm that Divine love is expressing through those who are closest to the individual. In the case of children, give your mental treatments principally to those who surround them, such as the father, mother, or other relatives who are anxious and fearful about the children, by saying, "YOU FULLY AND FREELY RELEASE. YOU LOOSEN AND LET GO. YOU LET GO AND LET GOD. YOU FULLY AND FREELY GIVE FREEDOM TO THIS CHILD NOW."

---

1. See the chapter "The Healing Law of Release" in *The Dynamic Laws of Healing,* and the chapter, "Love Works a Healing Power" in *The Prospering Power of Love* (Marina del Rey: DeVorss & Co. 1966).

Little children are like mirrors. They reflect the thoughts and emotions of those nearest them, particularly the mother or the one who takes her place in their lives. If there is inharmony between the father and mother, or if they are in trouble in some way, the little ones are apt to show forth that condition through physical ailments and through behavior problems. Affirm that Divine love is being manifested in the parents as well as in the children. In his book, *A Parents' Guide to Emotional Needs in Children,*[2] Dr. David Goodman explains the psychological effects of parent relationships on their children's health and behavior.

The average person is not aware that he possesses the mighty power of love, which can neutralize every shaft of hate aimed at him. Love is a mind power native to man and exists in every one of us. It may be called forth and developed to bring about harmony among those who have been disunited through misunderstanding, contention or selfishness.

Certain words that are used persistently mold and transform conditions in mind, body, and affairs. The word "love" overcomes hate, resistance, opposition, anger, obstinancy, jealousy, and other possessive emotions that produce mental and physical friction.

Words make cells and these cells are related to one another through associated ideas. When Divine love enters into man's thought processes, every cell becomes poised, balanced, harmonious, and attuned to the entire organism. *Words of love have a balancing effect upon the mind and body.*

---

2. David Goodman, *A Parents' Guide to Emotional Needs in Children* (New York: Hawthorn Books, Inc., 1959).

HOW TO HANDLE CRITICISM IN HEALING

I recently saw a placard in an airport which read, "Love your enemies. It drives them nuts!" Sometimes it even drives them sane.

As related in my book *The Dynamic Laws of Prosperity*, a businessman had a special way of handling critical people: he shot them in the back—but with love!

There is a way you can retain your own sanity, too, amid criticism. When someone is angry with you and fault is found, instead of beginning to defend yourself answering back in the same spirit, say to yourself: "DIVINE LOVE IS AT WORK. NONE OF THESE THINGS MOVE ME. THIS TOO SHALL PASS." As you hold to these thoughts, *two things will happen."*

First, you will begin to realize that the angry fault-finding has no effect upon you. *Secondly,* you will find that the attacks of criticism become less bitter, less frequent, until they cease altogether.

When you observe other people as victims of condemnation, declare for them: "DIVINE LOVE IS AT WORK PROTECTING YOU NOW. NONE OF THESE THINGS MOVE YOU. THIS TOO SHALL PASS." In this way love can neutralize criticism and its destructive results.

Fault-finding and condemnation cause all kinds of illness, whereas, when you speak words of praise, love or kindness to a person or for him, you help clear up diseases that have been caused by condemnation.

A woman was once healed of a cataract on her eye when a friend decreed for her: "I PRONOUNCE YOU FREE FROM THE CRITICISM OF OTHERS. YOU THINK YOUR OWN NOBLE THOUGHTS. I PRONOUNCE YOU WELL, STRONG AND AT PEACE THROUGH AND THROUGH."

HOW TO HANDLE THE HEALING PROCESS OF LOVE

People in public life have actually been killed by having criticisms hurled at them. If they had known how to protect themselves through speaking words of love both for themselves and their critics, they could have neutralized the condemnation and its deadly effects.

Anytime you find yourself in the midst of fault-finding, call on Divine love to deliver you. It can transform every inharmony, heal disease, transmute negative conditions into harmonious ones. *Love is healing energy!*

If you feel a lack of satisfaction in your life, if the way seems hard, it is an indication that you should be calling forth the mind power of love from within you. It can do wonderful things for and through you, as it smooths your path, replaces friction with harmony, dissolves tension, and sends its healing currents through your entire body. You will also find it an irresistible magnet for satisfying your emotional needs and manifesting substance as increased financial supply.

As you begin to meditate upon Divine love, it comes alive in the heart and lung area. It will flow through your body temple, cleansing, purifying, and harmonizing it. It will flow through your emotional nature, quickening a feeling of love there and bringing peace of mind. It will flow into your relationships as understanding and harmony. As you begin thinking of yourself as a radiating center of Divine love, you shall find that love has made you a magnet, attracting good to you from all directions, pleasantly changing your world. With Solomon you may even chant, "My ways are ways of pleasantness, and all my paths are peace." (Proverbs 3:17)

For this purpose, turn your thoughts to the heart area

as you relax and declare often: "I AM THE PERFECT EX-PRESSION OF DIVINE LOVE." Make this your basic affirmation for developing your mind power of love. Then in your quiet times, also use some of the following statements: "LOVE TRANSFORMS. LOVE TRANSFIGURES. LOVE FILLS MY HEART WITH HARMONY. LOVE FILLS MY MIND WITH KIND, HELPFUL THOUGHTS. LOVE FILLS MY LIPS WITH WORDS OF PRAISE AND CHEER. LOVE FILLS MY LIFE TO OVERFLOW-ING WITH HAPPINESS AND PEACE. WHATEVER THE NEED OR PROBLEM, DIVINE LOVE IS THE ANSWER, AND I AM THE PERFECT EXPRESSION OF DIVINE LOVE. DIVINE LOVE NOW FULFILLS MY EVERY NEED."

The person who has learned how to make union with Divine love through his inner consciousness, who lets its healing current flow into his soul and body, is fortunate beyond description.

LUNGS, BREAST, CHEST AFFECTED BY LACK OF LOVE

Any disturbance of the affections unbalances one's health, especially affecting the lungs, breast, and chest area. Hurts in the love nature are especially reflected as disease in these areas.

In his book, *Psychology, Religion and Healing,*[3] Dr. Leslie Weatherhead pointed out that the deprivation of love is the main factor behind many physical illnesses. However, as one begins developing and radiating the mind power of love from within outward, it opens the way for love's emotional and physical fulfillment to mani-fest in the body. For such purposes affirm: "MY BODY DOES NOT STARVE FOR MY LOVE AND APPRECIATION OF IT.

---

3. Leslie D. Weatherhead, *Psychology, Religion and Healing* (New York—Nashville, Tenn.: Abingdon Press).

I RECOGNIZE ITS IMPORTANCE, HONOR IT, AND LOVE IT AS
THE TEMPLE OF THE LIVING GOD!"

Lack of love, at the seat of the emotions affects not
only the action of the heart, but also the lungs as an extension of the heart. In fact, the movements of the heart
and lungs determine the movements of all organs of the
body. These organs, located in the thorax area of the
chest, are connected with all other organs through the
sympathetic nervous system.

THE THYMUS GLAND ASSOCIATED
WITH MAN'S LOVE NATURE

The thymus gland is also situated in the chest. It
covers the upper portion of the heart and is situated behind the breastbone. A gland of mystery, it is physically
thought to relate to nutrition and growth, and probably

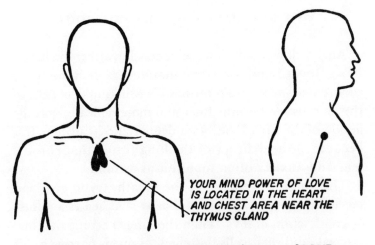

YOUR MIND POWER OF LOVE
IS LOCATED IN THE HEART
AND CHEST AREA NEAR THE
THYMUS GLAND

Figure 5–1.   Location of the Mind Power of LOVE.

to one's emotional development in the early phases of life. Scientific studies reveal a possible link between the malfunctioning of the thymus gland and a number of diseases, such as rheumatoid arthritis, leukemia, and other unusual blood disorders.

Metaphysically, the thymus gland, being closely situated to the heart, is associated with man's love nature. A malfunction of this gland indicates a malfunction of the mind power of love located in that area.

On the Greek temples of old were written, "Love tempered with wisdom is the secret of life." This can certainly be the secret of health. Love and wisdom united result in quick intuitional knowing, while love acting independently of wisdom may bring unpleasant results. Love alone may be impulsive, but united with wisdom, it always intuitively knows the wise course, so that discordant conditions of mind and body can be harmonized. For this purpose affirm: *Divine love and wisdom are united in me.*

WHY BASE PASSIONS ARE DANGEROUS

Anger, ill will, and intense depression affect the heart, lungs, breath and sometime manifest as pneumonia or tuberculosis. As a man refines his thinking, the cells of the lung-tissues become finer and more delicate, and the action of the breath becomes deeper and healthier. It is because of the delicacy of the lung tissues that chronic fear and anxiety often manifest as asthma.

The lungs, as vehicles of the breath, try to give and receive love freely. Disease in that area indicates a misuse or constriction of love. Then the lungs become narrow, warped, and their cells flattened, as one is narrow in his love, thinking it to be limited to possessive attitudes of "mine and thine."

When love is selfish and does not seek to protect and nourish, it will outpicture as disease in the breast or chest area. Also, this part of the body seems to need an assurance of protection. Disease appears in the chest or breast when it feels unprotected or when it possessively attempts to protect another, and conflict results.

A dominating mother who had reared her children alone, and resented the husband whose desertion had left her to do so, then tried to compensate for that lack of love through possessiveness of her sons. She became very upset when they married, criticized their wives, and insisted that her sons visit her alone. In her jealousy, she insisted their wives were not "good enough" for them. (The usual cry of possessive mothers!)

The ultimate result was that one son landed in a mental institution. The other son suffered from a lung disease which reflected his mother's "smothering love."

But this misguided mother suffered the greatest damage of all, through cancer of the breast which later spread into the shoulders. The shoulder indicates responsibility, and malignancy there indicated a malignant holding on to adult children whom she should have long since released.

Although she affirmed healing and others prayed with her, she continued condemning her daughters-in-law, even refusing to see them during her last illness. At the time of her death one son was still in a mental hospital, but it was amazing how quickly he recovered once he was emotionally released from his mother's possessiveness.

Not so for a daughter who had been abnormally attached to her possessive mother. She grieved and resented her mother's death so much that within a year she also had to have a breast removed. Part of her trouble also lay in resentment toward her husband who had patiently endured his dominating mother-in-law, even when she had pitted him against his wife. His wife wished that he and not her mother had been taken from her. (Disease in any of the sex organs usually indicates resentment toward some member of the opposite sex.)

A HEALING OF BREAST CANCER

A malignant growth indicates anger, sensitiveness, impatience, bitterness or resistance. A person with a growth should determine to love his worst enemies — which are his own malignant thoughts. He should give up every sense of injury which has settled in the sensitive nerves of the breast and lungs. "NOTHING HURTS IN SPIRIT. THERE IS NOTHING TO FEAR BECAUSE THERE IS NO POWER TO HURT."

A woman with breast cancer visited a spiritual counselor. One breast had already been removed and the other had been operated on. In fact, she had had several agonizing operations for cancer in other parts of the body, too. If she did not find healing immediately, she would die because the poison had now spread throughout her system.

The counselor told her she must spend time each day quietly forgiving everything and everybody, including herself. Whatever she had strong feelings for or against she must forgive. "CHRIST NOW HEALS ME OF ALL SENSE OF HURT, INJURY, OR BITTERNESS. LOVE IS ALL THERE IS IN MY MIND AND HEART. I PUT ON THE BREASTPLATE OF RIGHT- EOUSNESS. I CAST ALL SENSE OF INJURY, HURT, RESENTMENT UPON THE CHRIST WITHIN, WHICH SETS ME FREE. WHILE I

AM SPEAKING, EVERY CELL HEARS MY CALL AND RESPONDS TO THE POWER OF DIVINE LOVE, NOW RELEASED IN ME."

The hard lump in her breast disappeared, as the little cells around the growth stopped nourishing it and closed up. For lack of nourishment, the cancer later came out of its socket, just as a nut comes out of a shell, leaving clean, new, pure flesh underneath as she affirmed: "EVERY PLANT, WHICH MY HEAVENLY FATHER HATH NOT PLANTED, SHALL BE ROOTED UP. THERE IS NOTHING IN ME TO FEED A FALSE GROWTH."

Through such attitudes and expressions of love, this woman had put on "the breastplate of faith and love" (I Thessalonians 5:8) of which Paul wrote. Healing of the breast was the literal result. Later, after a thorough examination by her doctor, he said, "I cannot find even a trace of cancer in you. You have been thoroughly healed." In her happiness she continued affirming: "LOVE HAS HEALED ME OF EVERY FALSE THOUGHT AND DESIRE. HENCEFORTH, LOVE SHALL FOREVER THINK THROUGH ME."

Many chronic diseases are manifested upon the body because of some secret rankling in the feeling nature of a person which results in unforgiveness. Love and forgiveness are the two great solvents in the heart of man that dissolve gallstones, cancers, tumors, and other diseases that are often considered incurable. New thoughts make new cells. Loving thoughts make curable cells!

For this purpose affirm: "I DISMISS FROM MY MIND AND BODY ALL SENSE OF INJURY. I LET DIVINE LOVE MANIFEST IN ME NOW."

AN ENLARGED HEART IS HEALED

The heart as the great love center in the body is the fountain of the most sensitive feelings. A businessman had poured out his adoration upon his wife, who reciprocated his love until taken from him through death. He was completely lost. There was a shutting down of his love nature and soon doctors said he had a dangerously enlarged heart. There was shortness of breath, weakness, and pain. Because of this condition, he was told he must be very quiet most of the time.

Because he had confined his love by putting a fence around it, enlargement of the physical heart had been the natural result. Healing of this type often comes when some object or activity is found upon which the person can express his love nature in service, thus drawing him out of himself.

This suffering man's minister said to him: "You can never be separated from God's love which was expressed in your life through love for your wife. God's love will continue to find ways to express for you. Do not think that love has failed you. Instead, thank God that you have loved and been loved. 'Tis better to have loved and lost than never to have loved at all.' Call on divine love to meet your every need and it will."

As he began affirming: "THERE IS ONLY LOVE IN MY HEART FOR EVERYONE. I POUR OUT MY LOVE TO ALL MANKIND. I SUPPRESS OR HOARD NOTHING. I WILL LET GOD FREELY LOVE THROUGH ME NOW AND ALWAYS," within a few weeks he had been healed of all physical discomfort and his heart became normal again in size.

WHAT LOVE CAN DO FOR YOU

Relax—and call on Divine love often. You can develop the mind power of love, located in the heart area, as you breath deeply and meditate upon words of love. This simple process can completely transform your health in the heart-lungs-chest-breast area of the body. And, you may even notice a complete transformation taking place in every phase of your world as well![4]

4. See the chapter, "The Healing Law of Love" in *The Dynamic Laws of Healing*; the chapter, "The Prosperity Law of Love and Good Will" in *The Dynamic Laws of Prosperity*; the chapter "Prosperity Through the Love Concept" in *Open Your Mind to Prosperity*; and the book, *The Prospering Power of Love*, all by Catherine Ponder.

Your healing faculty of

POWER

— 6 —

An Oriental fable tells of the ancient gods trying to decide where to hide the power of the universe, so that man would not find it and use it destructively.

One god said, "Let us hide it on top of the highest mountain." But they decided that man would eventually scale the highest mountain and find this great power.

Another god said, "Let us hide this power at the bottom of the sea." Again it was decided that man would eventually explore the depths of the sea.

Still a third god suggested, "Let us hide the great power of the universe in the middle of the earth." But they realized that man would someday conquer that region, too.

Finally the wisest god of all said, "I know what to do. Let us hide the great power of the universe *within* man. He will never think to look for it there!"

According to this old fable, they *did* hide the power of the universe within man, and it is still there. Furthermore, they were right. Few people have ever realized that the great power of the universe—the power to kill or cure—lies within themselves.

POWER CENTER IN THE THROAT

This great power of the universe not only lies within man, but has a definite location in the throat in a brain center at the root of the tongue. Through this brain center, the mind faculty of power controls the larynx, tongue, tonsils, and all the organs used in forming words.

The power center in the throat is located near the thyroid gland, just below the Adam's apple at the base of the neck, astride of the windpipe as shown in Figure 6-1. *This powerful thyroid gland controls the metabolism of energy in the body. In fact, the mind*

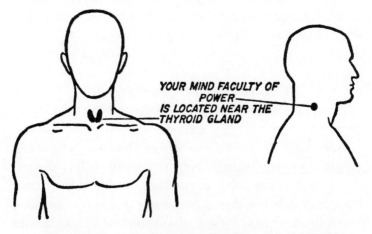

Figure 6–1.   Location of the Mind Faculty of POWER.

faculty of power located in this thyroid gland in the throat controls all the vibratory energies of the body. Once you know this, it is easy to see the power that your words have to produce health or disease. It is also easy to see how your words react upon the power center in the throat.

Words of condemnation can produce a scratchy or sore throat. Irritating words often produce an irritated cough. Willfulness leads to confusion and confusion causes colds and other throat and chest diseases.

Your mind faculty of power operates through a large group of nerves in the throat that control the larynx or voice box. You can harness the power within you and begin directing it constructively by harnessing your words or "watching your tongue." Incidentally, the tongue is closely related to the soul nature.

Also, the literal creative power of the thyroid gland, as the metaphysical center of the mind faculty of power, is shown in the fact that in ancient times the thyroid gland was considered a sex gland, frequently described as "the third ovary." Even in modern times, when a woman has ovarian trouble, it is often an indication that she has created it through negative words.

THE TREMENDOUS EFFECT OF
WORDS ON BODY AND MIND

Since ancient times the power of one's words has been taught and emphasized. Negative words affect the entire body, but are prone to produce trouble in the throat area, from whence they came; whereas, happy, life-filled words produce health throughout the body, especially in the throat area.

The body feeds on man's words. When those words

are life-giving, they are health-producing. Every time you speak, you cause the atoms of your body to tremble and change their place. Not only do you cause the atoms of your own body to change their position, but as you mentally raise or lower the rate of your own vibrations, you also affect the bodies of other people with whom you come in contact, just as they do you.

This explains why you often feel tired, depressed and physically run down after being in the company of negative-speaking people.

Every word brings forth after its kind — first in mind, then in body, and later in the affairs of the individual. The usual conversations among most people create ill health instead of good health, because of wrong words.

When words are spoken that describe disease as a reality, those words unconsciously set in motion disintegrating forces in the body which shatter the strongest organism if they are not counteracted by constructive words.

For instance, talking about nervousness and weakness will produce those conditions in the body; whereas, sending forth the word of strength and affirming life can help produce strength in the desired part of the body.

An example is that of a mother telling a little child that he looks sick and tired, thereby producing those conditions in the child's mind and body; whereas, if that mother spoke words of health, life, and strength to the child, these would set his bodily functions reacting normally.

WHY YOU SHOULD CLOSELY CONTROL YOUR VOICE

You should control your voice most carefully. It has a far greater effect on your health and nervous system than you have ever suspected, as well as affecting the nerves and health of those about you.

It has been observed by students of the mind that words of love, faith, and harmony spoken from the heart enrich the voice, tone up the vocal cords, soothe and heal laryngitis, cleanse and restore the tonsils that may be swollen and diseased.

You can tell a lot about a person's state of mind by his voice. An inharmonious voice indicates an inharmonious state of mind. Avoid such people whenever possible, since they have nothing to add to your own health, wealth or happiness, and in their present state of mind they are invariably tearing down their own.

It is easy to believe that a voice in an angry, rasping dispute irritates the throat and nasal passages. A housewife became very upset with her husband. During a quarrel she shouted loud words of criticism at him. Within two minutes she had produced a diseased condition that manifested within two hours as a "bad cold," which she then spent two weeks trying to get rid of! Many of us generate diseased conditions in the throat area and throughout the body, through methods just as simple and foolish as that. As Isaiah pointed out, "Woe unto them that decree unrighteous decrees." (Isaiah 10:1)

To avoid this, declare often: "I SPEAK NO WORDS OF EVIL. I DO NOT BELIEVE IN REPEATING UNPLEASANT WORDS. I FORGIVE THOSE WHO SPEAK EVIL FOR THEY KNOW NOT WHAT THEY DO. I SPEAK ONLY GOOD FOR I KNOW THE POWER OF MY WORDS TO CREATE WHATEVER I DECREE."

As for the power that our voice and words have upon another, many years ago a boy of seven was healed of mastoiditis by his grandmother. This was in the days before modern medications, when an elderly woman in the family often acted as nurse and substitute-doctor.

When asked how she had healed her grandson, she later explained: "I prayed through the night as I worked over him. He had not been able to hear for several days and doctors feared that he might never hear again. He was in a very critical condition. I asked that the voice of the Good Shepherd might speak through me and that Bobby might hear that voice and answer it by getting well."

This little seven-year-old boy later described his healing: "Grandma's voice was like the sound of running water. First it stopped the burning in my head, then it made my earache better. Then I heard her call my name and I answered her."

You can build into your voice so great a measure of peace and harmony that it will become a healing influence to anyone who hears it. It will prove a blessing to you and to those about you.

You can begin by letting go of ill temper, hasty, scolding words, rasping tones. When you let these negative attitudes go, you are well on the way to letting go of the inharmonies they cause in the throat area, such as swollen tonsils, annoying sinus trouble, throat irritations, and nasal disturbances.

The power of words to kill or to cure is so important that I have written about it in several other books, and suggest that you study the chapters in them pertaining to the power of the word.[1]

---

1. See *The Dynamic Laws of Healing,* Chapter 5; *The Dynamic Laws of Prosperity,* Chapter 6; *The Prosperity Secrets of the Ages,* Chapter 2; *Open Your Mind to Prosperity,* Chapter 5; *Open Your Mind to Receive,* Chapter 3; and *Pray and Grow Rich,* Chapter 6.

SOME HEALINGS RESULTING FROM
THE POWER OF WORDS

Included among the many stories in these books which point out how your words kill or cure is that in which a nurse talked her son back to health when he was at death's door.

This teenager, very ill, was placed in a room with two other patients, neither of whom was expected to live. In this depressed atmosphere, he grew weaker and weaker, despite the finest medical treatment.

This mother employed the help of all attending her son — his nurses, doctors and hospital attendants — asking that they daily speak encouraging words to him about his recovery. Not only did he recover, but the other two patients in his room also got well!

Later one of these patients told the boy: "Your mother not only talked you back to life, but her words gave me new hope and new life also. Had it not been for your mother's daily words of encouragement, I believe we would both be dead today."

The great ancient metaphysician Solomon wrote: "A cheerful heart causeth good health. But a broken spirit drieth up the bones." (Proverbs 17:22)

Some months ago, an educator from the New England states related how she was healed while talking with a minister, who employed the healing power of words.

In pain from arthritis, this educator was vacationing in Florida in an effort to regain her health. There she visited the minister and asked for prayers for her health. As she sat listening to this minister's soothing voice state that God's will for her was health, that pain and disease were unnecessary, she relaxed so much that she fell asleep in her chair. After a short nap she awakened refreshed to find the pain gone. The arthritic condition that faded that day has never returned.

Dr. G. LeRoy Dale was a great believer in the healing power of words, and it was in his famous metaphysical "exercise classes" that I was first introduced to the power of spoken affirmations many years ago.

Friends of mine once attended a five-day spiritual retreat at beautiful Unity Village. Upon their return I asked what had impressed them most. It was the following incident:

While strolling in the Unity rose garden one day, they observed a man suddenly fall upon the ground with an epileptic seizure. Dr. Dale quickly appeared and began decreeing in a loud voice: *"In the name of Jesus Christ, you are healed! Arise and walk."* Quietly the man arose as the seizure faded, and he walked away.

Power is released by merely stating words of life, health, vitality. The body can be renewed, even transformed through the spoken word. Owing to the vibratory power of words, whatever man decrees, that he releases within himself and within his world.

AN ANCIENT HEALING METHOD
WITH SPOKEN WORDS

One of the great secrets of Mr. and Mrs. Fillmore's healings, as related in Chapter 1, was their persistent use of spoken words of life and power. I once heard a worker at Unity School of Christianity recall the time he walked into Charles Fillmore's office for advice on some matter, and Mr. Fillmore was saying a healing affirmation. The worker patiently waited while Mr. Fillmore continued saying the healing statement. When he had finished, the worker asked, "How many times have you affirmed that statement this morning?" Mr. Fillmore's reply was, "I just finished decreeing it two thousand times!"

The spoken words of life, health, and power working through the thyroid gland in the throat stir up tremendous energy in the body. Both the ancient Egyptians and Brahmins knew this, and used spoken words of healing to set up a vibratory reaction which dispelled congestion and helped nature restore broken bones and depleted organs.

In ancient times when there were no doctors and non-medical methods of healing had to be used, the spoken word often healed. The priest-physicians knew about the dynamics of sound and realized that every spoken word had tremendous power. By certain arrangements of words, such as in healing affirmations, a tremendous vibratory force could be set upon in the invisible which profoundly affected physical substance in the body of man.

The priests knew that by their persistent healing chants, they greatly stimulated the 12 mind powers located in vital nerve centers in the body, deliberately activating and releasing increased energy into all parts of the body. Healing was the natural result.

In India, it is both legend and tradition that the sung or spoken word is 80 percent more powerful than silent words of Truth. When a person tells you his health was restored by "spiritual treatment," he means it was restored through spoken words. A spiritual treatment is a truth *spoken,* a healing idea *stated.* Diseases can be completely wiped out of consciousness through spoken words.

The late Florence Shinn constantly taught that your word is your wand to wave over your life and make it what you will. From a prominent Philadelphia family, Mrs. Shinn was a well-known artist before becoming a metaphysician. Her famous little book, *The Game of Life and How to Play It*,[2] relates countless demonstrations of Truth made by people simply speaking words.

If you've been inclined to underestimate the power of healing through the spoken word, perhaps it would help for you to know about a prominent metaphysician, who charged $500 for a half-hour consultation and always had a waiting list! His method of healing? Affirmation!

WHAT TO DO WHEN YOU FEEL POWERLESS IN COPING WITH DISEASE

When you feel powerless before some diseased appearance, remind yourself that strong, *firmly held thoughts in your mind actually change your body's chemistry*. Thoughts of intense, negative emotion cause a short-circuit in your nervous system, depleting your muscles of energy and lead to a breakdown in circulation, digestion, and elimination activities in the body.

Remind yourself that thoughts of hate can cook the corpuscles in the blood, which may be the real cause of cancer and tumors. Boiling thoughts of rage and jealousy explode the body system and release dangerous poisons into the heart and stomach areas. Thoughts of bitterness and condemnation shrivel the cells of the body, harden veins and arteries, and congest the flow of life fluids throughout the body system. This leads to paralysis, arthritis, and rheumatism.

---

2. Florence Scovel Shinn, *The Game of Life and How to Play It* (Marina del Rey, CA.: De Vorss & Co., 1925).

Much of what has been called disease and sickness results from feeding the mind and body on empty, destructive, lifeless words. Such words have no vitality in them and leave a vacuum in the mind, as well as a devitalizing feeling of emptiness in the body.

We have often heard it said that man has a new body at least once a year. This being true, it seems strange that year after year there should be an increasing appearance of ill health and age in most people. The cause is man's ignorant use of words. Japanese metaphysician Dr. Masaharu Taniguchi, who has been so successful in healing cancer, explains: "Prejudices and resentments must go. Fault-finding and criticism cannot co-exist with health. Man must practice forgiveness to remain healthy."[3]

Instead of building new cells with life-filled words, man usually builds disease and age into them through his destructive words. *If man's destructive words did not interfere with the body-building process, they would build a perfect body and keep it in perfect order!* As Dr. Alexis Carrel has written: "Those people who keep the peace of the inner self in the midst of turmoil are immune to both nervous and organic disorders."[4]

The mind faculty of power located in the throat is found in the area of the conscious mind. This means that you can consciously and deliberately activate power, life, and vitality through your spoken words. Power has been described as the ability to start things, such as new streams of life, health, vitality flowing into the body.

Quietly speaking words of life and love to every cell

---

3. Masaharu Taniguchi, *You Can Heal Yourself* (Tokyo, Japan: Seicho-no Ie Foundation, 1961).

4. *Man, The Unknown* (New York: Harper & Row, 1935).

and organ and function of the body is the sure and permanent way to change your thought habits and bring about improved bodily health, along with new strength, new bone structure, new cell tissues, enriched blood supply, and a toning up of the whole organism within and without. *If you wish to heal yourself, talk to your mind and body as you would talk to a patient.*

The word "utter" and the word "outer" have the same root meaning. What you "utter" becomes "outer" in your body and affairs! Knowing this you need no longer feel powerless if disease strikes. You can do as the housewife who wrote:

> "Whenever anything happens in my life that I feel powerless to cope with, *I loose my voice on it.* Often I have to put great feeling into my affirmations (speaking them in a loud voice stirs up the feeling nature and emotions), in order to gain a sense of dominion and authority. At such times I like to affirm: 'I AM A CHILD OF GOD AND HAVE DOMINION OVER ALL THE CONDITIONS IN MY LIFE NOW. POWER, POWER, POWER IS MINE NOW!'"

A businessman recently stated that meditating upon the word "power" had proved the turning point from failure to success in his financial affairs. Once when he was praying for guidance, the thought came to him, "Ask and speak with authority, and I will give you the power." He followed that guidance and as he went forth into his business life acting and speaking with authority, it was as though fresh new power came to him. He bought a car at his price on his terms. He negotiated various business deals to the mutual benefit of all involved. He was guided to a business partner and, thereafter, to fresh new business after he acted and spoke with dominion and power.

My son once summarized the success of a famous prizefighter who always acted and spoke with authority: "He has won 22 championship fights 'with his mouth.'"

Man's body is filled with innate intelligence. Through speaking words of confidence and power over and over, man gains conscious attention of the intelligence within the organs of his body. As he continues to speak words of power, that innate intelligence is tapped and it releases increased life and substance into the mind, body and affairs of man.

Out in Hawaii, a woman had been in the hospital three months suffering from cancer. A pathetic sight, she was down to only 60 pounds when a minister visited her. He said to her, "You can die if you want to, but God wants you to be healed. All power is yours to regain your health." She spoke aloud these words with him: "GOD WANTS ME TO BE HEALED. ALL POWER IS MINE TO REGAIN MY HEALTH."

He did not hear from her again for three months, but when he did, she was at home, 40 pounds heavier and recovering nicely.

THE DISEASE-CAUSING POWER OF WORDS

People who continually speak of disease invariably attract it. Knowing this, a person cannot be too careful of his words. Words that "run down" other people react upon the critic in the form of some "run-down" condition, such as ill health, financial, or family problems. Continual criticism is believed to produce rheumatism. It is also reported to cause unnatural deposits in the blood which settle in the joints. People who suffer disease in their "joints" are usually people who are "out of joint" in their thinking! Unkind words will harden arteries, harden the liver, and affect the eyesight. Unforgiveness is a prolific cause of disease.

Destructive words cause endless ills. *Living in the past or complaining about your hard experiences in life also burdens your body with ill health. You release into your mind, body and affairs that which you think about and talk about. Your word is your power.*

Through the power center located in the throat, you create or destroy. Your words can dissolve obstacles and remove barriers; or your words can create obstacles and form barriers. It's up to you. People who suffer from obstructions in the body are people who first suffered from obstructions in their thinking. Usually they have felt that someone or some situation was an obstruction between them and their good.

A person should constantly speak words of life, health, vitality, and should raise his voice in constant praise. In this way he lifts his whole organism to a high, healthy, harmonious vibration, which reacts as good health in mind, body and affairs. *The body has natural forces within it that would transform it, if that power was consistantly released through constructive words!*

COMPLAINING WORDS LEAD TO
GOITER, PNEUMONIA, SURGERY

People who have throat troubles — goiter, false growths, tonsilitis, nervousness, excessive craving for food, undue emotionalism, throat irritations, and other thyroid disturbances — are usually quiet complainers. They may put up a good front to the world, but privately they are complaining about everything and everybody, and their complaints eventually react as disease in the throat.

A beautiful girl was suffering from a broken heart. Her fiancé had disappointed her by marrying someone else. Unable to talk about her disappointment to anyone, this girl expressed her unhappiness through complaints about many other things, such as her parents, their home to which she had returned, her job, relatives, etc.

In due time she developed a large goiter of the throat that finally had to be removed through a very serious operation, from which it took her months to recover.

Learning of the power of words, this young career woman analyzed her situation and realized she had misused her words; that false ideas had taken the shape of a false growth in the very area where those ideas had been expressed, and then had to be cut out. She vowed to "cut out" of her speech the mental equivalent that had caused that false growth: the words and ideas of limitation. Thus, her bout with ill health had not been in vain since she had learned to watch her words as a result.

For a number of years I puzzled over a lady who had the same health problem every spring. It would begin with a cold and sore throat and then would develop into pneumonia for which she would have to be hospitalized for many weeks, and from which she slowly recovered over a period of several months.

This lady had always put up a happy front to her relatives and friends, but I finally learned her true situation, which helped explain her yearly illnesses. Her husband had passed on several years previously, leaving her considerable wealth. But instead of giving her the money outright, he had arranged for a son-in-law to control the estate and handle all her business affairs.

She did not trust this son-in-law, and feared he was

misappropriating her funds. Every spring he would wait until the last minute to have her income taxes figured. As the deadline neared, he would rush in for her to sign the tax return, not allowing her time to check it over properly.

Instead of having her attorney quietly straighten out the situation, this lady would become emotionally upset and privately fume about this matter, beginning months before the tax deadline. As that deadline approached, she went through her "annual routine" emotionally, which led to pneumonia. What a high price she paid for not exerting dominion over her words as well as over her financial affairs.

Those quiet, private words you speak, often affect your mind, body and affairs much more than anything else you do, say, or think. Indeed, your every word is recorded in the body. Your words become your flesh. Every word when spoken, vibrates throughout your whole body and moves every cell and atom of your being. Repetition of any word fixes it in mind and causes it to become a moving force in the body. All power is given unto you in mind and body through your words!

Sometimes you see the power of destructive words work throughout an entire family group, such as the one in which both the husband and wife were "quiet complainers." For years this well-meaning couple had complained about everything, such as their careers, financial affairs, children, families, each other, and life in general.

During a routine check-up the wife learned one day she had a malignant growth in her throat. An operation was necessary. Shortly, her husband learned he, too, had a serious growth in his mouth which also required surgery.

This couple realized afterwards that this surgery was a warning to them to change what they were privately thinking and saying day in and day out, to stop complaining and to start seeing the good in themselves, each other, their marriage, careers, children, family and the world generally. Their deliberate change of words had made a great difference in their health and in their financial and family affairs. Everything has improved in their lives since they improved their thoughts and spoken words. A fine healing statement to help you along this line is: "VAST IMPROVEMENT COMES QUICKLY IN EVERY PHASE OF MY LIFE NOW."

A HEALING OF GOITER IS
EXPERIENCED THROUGH WORDS

A sensitive man, who was easily moved and disturbed by the words and deeds of others, developed a large goiter which lay on the side of his neck.

Being warned by doctors that an operation would be dangerous because of the size and type of goiter he had, this troubled man sought out a spiritual counselor, who soon got at the emotional cause of the false growth.

This sensitive man had a brother he could not stand, for he was dishonest in all his business dealings, continually doing and saying unkind and untrue things. This sensitive man had begged his brother to live a better life; but the brother only laughed and replied with impudent remarks. This man had lived in this miserable atmosphere for years as the inharmony between them had only grown worse.

The spiritual counselor explained to this sensitive man that he had felt powerless and that the powerless feeling had manifested itself as a false growth in the area of power at the neck. The counselor assured this man he could be healed through exerting his power in spoken words and suggested he constantly affirm: "I LOVE YOU WITH THE LOVE OF CHRIST, AND YOU LOVE ME WITH THE LOVE OF CHRIST. LOVE MELTS ALL INHARMONY BETWEEN US. LOVE NOW GIVES US PERFECT PEACE. LOVE IS ALL POWERFUL TO PRODUCE HEALING NOW. LOVE WINS!"

It took two months of persistently speaking these words daily, but it worked. The goiter on the man's neck gradually went away. Also, another healing occurred as these two brothers were reconciled and, thereafter, lived in harmony and peace.

SHE TALKS THEM BACK TO HEALTH

Perhaps you have heard the colloquial expression, "She nearly talked me to death." You can literally talk a person to death or to life. A southern housekeeper had a number of experiences along this line. Several years ago she was asked to nurse a wealthy, elderly widow who was so lonely for her deceased husband that she had given up the will to live. After she had been in the hospital a number of weeks, her doctors were mystified as to the cause of her illness and kept changing their diagnosis. Finally they agreed that she had symptoms of cancer.

After weeks of no improvement, this woman's children decided in despair that she should go to the home of a daughter and there continue receiving medication. This daughter's housekeeper was a very positive person, and immediately began to speak words of life and health to the lonely widow.

Each morning the housekeeper would give her a warm, stimulating bath, and would tell her funny stories to purposely make her laugh and think about happy things. Within a month, all symptoms of illness were gone and all medication was stopped. All this happened several years ago and the mysterious illness has not recurred. The widow is now past 80 and continues to lead a very active life.

HOW TO LIBERATE THIS POWER OF WORDS

The universal life current is subject and obedient to the word of man. A great example of this was shown when Jesus raised Lazarus from the dead. Lazarus had been in the tomb four days and no doubt his body was disintegrating. But Jesus, knowing the power of the word to release atomic energy in every cell of Lazarus' body, deliberately released it through His spoken words.

When Jesus affirmed in a loud voice, "Lazarus, come forth," (John 11:43) Lazarus obeyed by coming forth, completely whole. Indications of the mighty healing power of the word are scattered throughout the Bible, but are especially found in the ministry of Jesus. Through the spoken word He performed seeming miracles.

The power center located at the root of the tongue has contact with the spiritual center at the crown of the head. It generates a healing power that flows to all parts of the body, when that healing power is released with good words. Think and speak sound, happy, constructive, life-filling words. They quickly tone up the mind and body, and make way for healings to occur.

There is mighty healing power stored up in the atoms

and cells of the body awaiting liberation. Concentrating upon the word "power" helps to liberate this mighty healing force, so that it may do its perfect work in the mind and body of man. Also, the mind faculty at the base of the brain known as "zeal" and the mind faculty located in the sex organs known as "life" are especially responsive to the spoken word of power. These mind faculties—power, zeal, and life—work closely together. Thus, through your spoken words of power, you release into these mind powers in vital areas of the body the greatest force in the universe—the conscious power of thought!

If you have health problems in the throat area—whether they have been caused by your own negative words or the negative words of others directed toward you—you can begin to release constructively the power found there by affirming: "ALL POWER IS NOW GIVEN ME IN MIND, BODY AND AFFAIRS. THE POWER OF GOD IS NOW WORKING THROUGH ME TO FREE ME FROM EVERY NEGATIVE INFLUENCE. NOTHING CAN HOLD ME IN BONDAGE. ALL POWER IS MINE TO CONTROL MY THOUGHTS, TO VITALIZE MY BODY, TO EXPERIENCE SUCCESS, AND TO BLESS OTHERS. I AM STRONG IN THE LORD AND IN THE POWER OF HIS MIGHT."

Among the apostles of Jesus, Philip symbolized the power faculty of the mind. The word "Philip" means "a lover of horses" and in physical activity the horse represents power.

Fortunately, man has the power to dissolve all discordant, disintegrating, disease-forming words. Knowledge of this truth is among the greatest discoveries of all ages! This means that you can make yourself a new creature, and you can build your world to your highest ideals. Do not fear appearances, problems, or diagnoses, but deliberately speak forth the desires of your heart privately.

Indeed, it is your duty as the beloved child of God to speak forth good words and manifest your innate perfection of health, wealth and happiness.

Realizing the creative power of words, the Psalmist decreed: "LET THE WORDS OF MY MOUTH, AND THE MEDITATIONS OF MY HEART BE ACCEPTABLE IN THY SIGHT, O LORD, MY STRENGTH, AND MY REDEEMER." (Psalms 19:14)

You may wish to join him in the use of this prayer often for healings.

Your healing power of

IMAGING

— 7 —

The famous Judge Thomas Troward once described the healing power of the imagination as follows: "Once you have seen the result you wish to attain, you have already willed a means that will take you to that result."

Your imagination is among your most creative mind powers. You are always creating through your imaging faculty. But, by deliberately directing your imagination toward what you want, you can begin to transform your health as well as every phase of your life. Again and again, your imaging power will gladly lead you into better living, once you invoke it.

Medical authorities have described the power of the imagination by explaining that *there are 20 times as many nerves running from the eyes to the brain, than from the ears to the brain*. Results come much quicker when you picture what you want, rather than just vaguely thinking or hearing about it.

In picturing health in the body, you are not trying to put something into the body that is not already there.

You are not trying to force the body into the mold of your own making. Instead, you are claiming and releasing the potential perfection, the "imprisoned splendor," that lies waiting to be recognized, released, and allowed expression in the cells of the body. Such mental action allows new forms to come forth so that "organic" healing occurs.

In his set of books, *Make Your Own World,*[1] Gordon Collier relates the fascinating story by John McDonald entitled "The Message of a Master" which emphasizes the healing power of the imagination.

A businessman was bankrupt and had such serious health problems that his doctor considered his case hopeless and ordered a trip to Europe as his last hope for recovery.

One night when he was contemplating suicide, this despondent business executive met a man in a London theater who simply called himself a "master." Within a month after their meeting, the previously dying businessman had returned home completely healed, and was also well on the way to making a fortune. Through private instruction, he had learned the secret of health, wealth, and happiness from that master whose formula included these ideas:

> "Any picture firmly held in mind, in any form, is bound to come forth. This is the great, unchanging Universal Law which, when we cooperate with it intelligently, makes us absolute masters of conditions and environment."

Through your thinking, you accumulate a mass of ideas and with your imagination you make them into

---

1. Gordon Collier, *Make Your Own World* (Tarrytown, N.Y.: Robert Collier Publications, Inc.).

definite forms. Your imagination is the "scissors of the mind" which takes your thoughts and gives them form.

LOCATION OF THE IMAGINATION

The front brain is the field of operation for the three closely connected mind powers discussed in this and the following chapters—imagination, understanding, and will.

Between the eyes is a ganglionic nerve center which, when deliberately quickened, will set into operation your imaging mind power. This is a point of expression for a set of tissues that extends back into the brain and connects with an imaging or picture-making function near the root of the optic nerve.

Through this mind power you can project an image of things that are without, or ideas that are within. For instance, you can project the image of jealousy to any part of your body, and by the chemistry of thought combined with physical functions, it will make your complexion appear yellow. Or you can image and project beauty and wholeness by thinking of goodness and perfection for yourself and others.

This imaging mind power is located in the vicinity of the pituitary gland which is about the size of a pea and lies at the base of the brain only a short distance behind the root of the nose. (See Figure 7-1.)

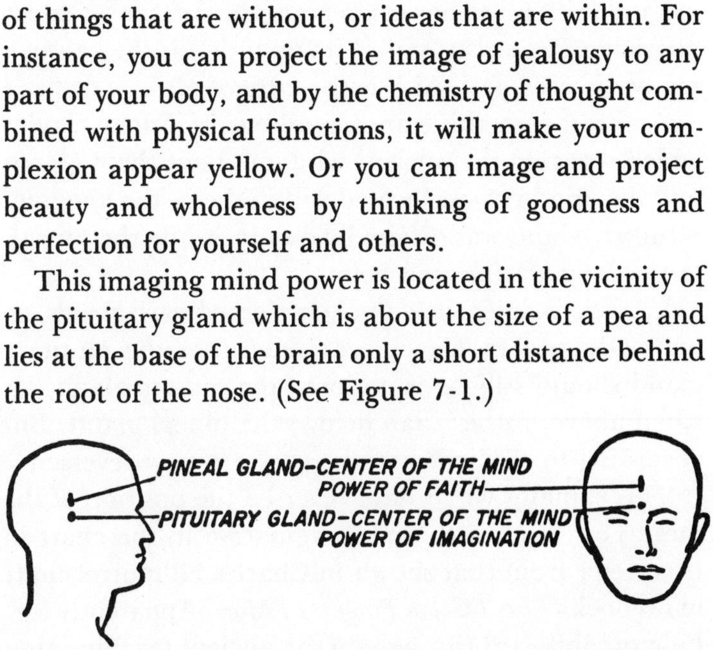

PINEAL GLAND—CENTER OF THE MIND POWER OF FAITH—

PITUITARY GLAND—CENTER OF THE MIND POWER OF IMAGINATION

Figure 7–1.   Location of the Mind Power of IMAGINATION.

Consisting of two glands in one, the pituitary is the gland of continuous effort. Where there is good pituitary development, there is strong mental activity and endurance. This gland affects both the emotional and mental nature of man. It affects sexual responses, certain muscular structures, and metabolism.

Since your imaging mind power extends back from the front forehead into the pituitary gland, this indicates that your mind power of imagination is closely connected with your faith faculty because the pituitary gland is located just under the pineal gland, which is the center of faith in the body. Thus, the mind powers of imagination and faith are closely connected in their mental action. What one constantly pictures, one has faith in and will manifest, whether it be health or disease, good or evil. Realizing the close connection between the imaging and faith mind powers in man, the sixteenth century physician Paracelsus said: "Imagination is the cause of many diseases, but faith is the cure of all."

According to the trance readings of Edgar Cayce, which revealed the ancient wisdom about these glands and the mind powers located within them, the imaging-pituitary gland was originally on top, while the pineal-faith gland was located below it.

In ancient times these were considered twin-glands. In his readings, Mr. Cayce contended that the pituitary gland should still be considered the master gland, located above, rather than below, the pineal gland. But according to medical science, they are now reversed.

This explains why I have reversed the position of the mind powers of faith and imagination in the chart in Chapter 1 from that shown in Charles Fillmore's chart in his book, *The Twelve Powers of Man*. Apparently Mr. Fillmore followed through on the ancient teaching that the pituitary-imagination gland is still located over the pineal-faith gland. But, according to modern science, these glands have reversed their positions.

The one thing of major importance, however, that stands out from the ancient teaching that the pituitary gland was originally located above the pineal gland is that your imaging power located in that gland is all important in your mental development. In these modern times, the fantastic power of the imagination is just now being rediscovered by modern psychologists, medical scientists, and metaphysicians. Regardless of their positions in the body, these twin mind powers—faith and imagination—are still meant to work closely together.

HEALTHY CHILD CONCEIVED AFTER IMAGING IT

Since the mind power of imagination is located between the eyes in the front brain and extends into the more interior regions of the brain, this indicates that it is located in the region of the conscious mind. This means that *through conscious use of your imagination, you can produce wonderful changes in your body and in every area of your life. The character of both your soul and body is affected by your imagination. The average person is yet to discover how powerful his imagination is.*

Dr. Phineas P. Quimby, father of mental and spiritual healing in America, wrote a century ago:

> "When people say, 'It's all your imagination,' they seem to mean it is nothing. On the contrary, imagination is probably the most powerful faculty of the human mind and thousands of practical men today know that what the mind images becomes experience and fact."[2]

---

2. *The Quimby Manuscripts* (New York: The Julian Press).

A Paris doctor once said:

> "It may indeed be all imagination and if it is, then imagination is a force as potent as it is little understood . . . If it can cure, is there any reason why we shouldn't use it? If Mesmer had discovered nothing more than that the imagination can exert a beneficial influence on health, would he not be one of our greatest physicians? His, I believe, is one of the most important discoveries at which the human mind has ever marveled."[3]

Your imagination is among the first of your latent mind powers to quicken. No matter what else you do or do not understand about the power of thought, *the imagination is a mind power that you can begin using immediately!* The more you practice developing this mind power, the more powerful your imagination will become. The more you train it to picture the good for yourself and others, the more quickly it will produce wonderful changes in your body and life.

Indeed, to picture the good is one of the most scientific, yet practical, ways of bringing it to pass. To picture healing is one of the quickest, easiest, and most pleasant ways of producing it metaphysically.

A housewife had been told she should not have another child, because she had lost one several years previously as a result of a toxic condition in the body. Upon learning of the healing power of the imagination, she decided to test it, through deliberately picturing a healthy pregnancy and a healthy child. (The wheel of fortune method she used is discussed later in this chapter.)

---

3. Ibid.

"Although I had lost a child as a result of a toxic condition a few years previously, I decided to make a wheel of fortune with pictures of beautiful perfect babies on it, placing this affirmative prayer under the pictures: 'THANK YOU FATHER. I AM TRUSTING.'

"I kept it in a convenient place and looked at it several times a day repeating the prayer statement often. Two months later my doctor confirmed that I was almost two months pregnant, and this time there were no signs of a toxic condition. In fact, this pregnancy was easy from the beginning. Each visit to the doctor brought good reports.

"During the previous pregnancy I had gained 30 pounds and had retained most of it afterwards. This time I gained only 10 pounds and within two weeks after the baby was born, had lost 23 pounds, making me 13 pounds lighter than before my pregnancy. This was a great blessing.

"Along with picturing a perfect pregnancy, delivery, and baby, I used certain affirmations which helped set up the image of health for me and for my child:

"Regarding my diet I affirmed, 'THROUGH THE POWER OF MY INDWELLING CHRIST, I THINK CONSTRUCTIVELY AND EAT WISELY. MY BODY IS BLESSED WITH ORDER AND HARMONY, AND I AM FREE FROM EXCESS WEIGHT.'

"Regarding any fear of the toxic condition returning, I declared: 'THE INFINITE LOVE OF GOD EVER ENFOLDS ME, BRINGING HARMONY, ORDER AND PEACE INTO MY MIND BODY AND AFFAIRS. NO NEGATIVE CONDITION CAN EXIST IN ME OR IN MY CHILD, ONLY GOOD NOW MANIFESTS IN ME AND IN MY CHILD.'

"In times of uneasiness I affirmed: 'GOD IS MY HEALTH, I CAN'T BE SICK. GOD IS MY STRENGTH, UNFAILING, QUICK.'

"Before each doctor's appointment I affirmed for my physician: 'YOU EXPRESS THE WISDOM, UNDERSTANDING AND HEALING TOUCH OF GOD.'

"Through labor and delivery, even under the anesthetic I used these affirmations: 'WITH EASE AND CONFIDENCE I BRING FORTH MY PERFECT CHILD. THERE IS NO PAIN. THERE IS NOTHING TO FEAR, THERE IS ONLY GOOD. GOD IS HERE AND ALL IS WELL.'

"For the doctors, nurses and hospital I declared: 'GOD'S GOOD IS WORKING THROUGH MY DOCTOR, NURSES, AND IN THIS HOSPITAL. THE CHRIST SPIRIT IS DOING ITS PERFECT WORK HERE AND ALL IS WELL.'"

Today this housewife is the healthy mother of a healthy baby.

MOTHER HEALS SON THROUGH IMAGING HIS PERFECT HEALTH

To picture the good for another person is one of the easiest and best ways of helping him to realize health and wholeness. So often a person thinks that the way to help another is by trying to talk to that person and convince him to accept and use certain ideas and techniques.

Usually that is the worst thing you can do. The person needing help then throws up a mental and emotional block. None of us wants to be told what to do by another. We all want to be free to find our own way, and rightly so.

Instead of trying to force other people to be helped in the way you think they should be, use the scientific, psychological and spiritual way which is to picture them whole in mind, body and affairs. Your happy pictures then reach past their emotional pride and intellectual argumentativeness right into their subconscious soul nature, which then gladly responds and silently works with you to produce happier results for them.

Experiments prove that we are constantly suggesting all sorts of things to one another and getting results according to the intensity of our imagination. *Picture a thing and bring it through, rather than trying to reason it through or force it through.*

A mother learned of the healing power of the imagination after her son had been ill most of the nine years of his life with a series of diseases. Despairing of medical help, this mother began a deep search for the mental laws of healing and discovered the imaging law. She realized that after his first illness or so, she had built up an image of sickness about her son, both in her mind and in his. Though she did not want him to be ill, she had expected him to be. Finally realizing this, she gratefully began changing her mental pictures and expectations concerning his health.

She began picturing him as the normal, healthy boy he should be. She imaged him as husky, rosy-cheeked, active and the "picture of health." She taught him to see himself the same way, as she helped him clip pictures of healthy children, teenagers, and young men to pin up on the walls of his room where he could view them often.

She quietly removed the thermometer and other medical items she had kept ready for use in his room. She spoke often of his return to perfect health. Together this mother and son planned for health and it came after nine years of continuous illness. His condition immediately improved and by the time he was in junior high school, this young man was a healthy, normal, busy boy in both school and church activities. He even excelled in sports. Later he attended college and did well.

PICTURING RAISES UP THE FORCES OF THE BODY

Jesus was describing the healing power of the imagination when He said, "The lamp of the body is the eye; if therefore thine eye be single, thy whole body shall be full of light." (Matthew 6:22)

When man's eye or imaging power is single or one-pointed toward health, the forces of his body are raised up. The currents of life begin to move upward as the creative energies ascend. As they move upward with new life and vigor, an increased strength and vitality begins to be felt.

Man is the only creature on earth that looks up! Where the forces of nature move upward, they always move with great energy and power.

As a person keeps his eye single to the picture of wholeness, a purification and freedom of limited pictures in the subconscious is released. New powers then awaken and move upward through his whole being, until a new life current has swept through his entire body. His mind is then quickened and his body revitalized. Solomon might have been describing this healing process when he said, "Where there is no vision, the people perish. But he that keepeth the law, happy is he." (Proverbs 29:18) "He that soweth iniquity shall reap calamity . . . He that hath a bountiful eye shall be blessed." (Proverbs 22:8,9)

Often we have cut off our good by thinking in strained terms of wishing, needing, wanting. Through the imaging power of the mind, we can begin to think in terms of having, being, and experiencing present fulfillment. This releases our good, quickens our energies and powers, and makes health an immediate possibility rather than a vague future hope.

SCHOOLTEACHER HEALED OF RASH

Whatever you can do to get other people picturing health for you is a powerful technique for producing it. For instance, when you are trying to get a healing, that is the time to put your best foot forward. This gives both yourself and others the impression of health.

When you are trying to get a healing, wear bright, light-colored clothes. The body seems to respond to bright colors, which suggest life, health, vitality.

A schoolteacher was suffering from an uncomfortable rash that had appeared after an automobile accident. Her doctor had not been able to relieve it. Through prayer with a spiritual counselor the rash would disappear, but then it would come back.

The counselor suggested she give thanks for perfect healing in a happy, joyous manner, and that she prepare for that healing by wearing her brightest, prettiest clothes every day until she was healed.

When her friends saw her dressed up, they assumed the rash was gone. She stopped mentioning it as she covered up the irritated areas with long-sleeved dresses and sweaters. Accepting dinner, party, and theater invitations again, she began going out and having a good time in spite of rash discomfort.

As she continued acting as though she was healed, everyone assumed she was and the rash gradually disappeared. Every time it tried to reappear, she would mentally say "no, no, no" to it as she again put on her brightest clothes and gaily had a good time. Finally the rash was healed completely and never returned. Later she surmised, "Wearing bright clothes helped me keep up my faith and courage, as well as suggesting to my friends that I was all right. It was such a simple method for invoking the imaging law of healing."

THE HEALING POWER OF COLOR AND MUSIC

Color healing was an ancient science and was practiced in the healing temples of Egypt, India and China. Our modern doctors and scientists are now rediscovering the power of color, and experiments have been made in some hospitals, showing how colors affect the patient's recovery. Particularly in mental hospitals is color healing found to be effective.

Also, when you are trying to relax and get the picture of healing working for you, music can be a great healer. Healing through music is another ancient art. In the Arab world, there was much healing done through music. The hospitals of the ancient world were far advanced over ours today. Often they were built in beautiful surroundings, amid spacious gardens. The hospital rooms were large and bright. Music was played to soothe the pain. That which adds beauty to your life also adds prospering, healing power.[4]

A NURSE HEALS ANOTHER
PERSON THROUGH IMAGING

A nurse once proved the fantastic healing power one can release for another person through constructive use of the imagination:

"I was working in surgery in a small hospital when an emergency arose. The other nurse, the orderly and I

---

4. See the chapter "The Success Power of Joy and Beauty," in *The Prosperity Secrets of the Ages;* and the chapter, "The Prosperity Law of Opulence," in *The Millionaire Moses.*

were taking a patient into the operating room for a very serious operation. As we transferred her from the stretcher onto the operating table, she stopped breathing. The two doctors in charge were on another floor. As we waited for them to arrive, I began to give the patient artificial respiration, but she was not responding.

"She appeared so lifeless on the table that I started praying for guidance. All at once I remembered the healing power of the imagination and said to the other nurse and to the orderly, 'This patient is a neighbor of mine. I know that she likes to bake bread and that she is well known for her wonderful homemade bread. Close your eyes and see her wearing an apron with dough in her hands, smiling and baking bread. The picturing power of the mind can heal her. Even if you do not agree, at least try this method.'

"I then went ahead mentally picturing the patient well again. 'Now she is buttering the pan in which she places the rolls. Her apron is pink, her dress is blue, and the kitchen is bright yellow. The bread pan is new and shiny as she places the rolls in it. I can now see her putting the pan of rolls in the oven and looking at the clock. Can you see her doing these things?'

"As I asked this question, the patient began to show signs of life, as she stirred, breathed deeply and became stronger. When the doctors arrived she was responding so well that they decided to go ahead with surgery. Her condition was a severe obstruction of the bowels, and the operation lasted three hours and 20 minutes.

"She stood it well, recovered completely, and soon went home. Furthermore, she baked the bread we had pictured and brought some of it to us at the hospital, as an act of appreciation. Although she was 80 years old at the time, she lived several more years in good health. When she talked about her operation later, she would say in a puzzled way, 'I felt like I was baking bread the whole time.' Of course, we never told her what had happened."

Since the imaging faculty is located between the eyes at the temples, people who concentrate too intensely may have headaches since they are trying to mentally force results. Your mind powers are like people. They can be praised and blessed into much activity, but they rebel against mental force with a negative reaction in the body. However, as you *gently* and serenely picture health, all of your five senses will respond and improve. Such health problems as excess weight, smoking and drinking respond to the picturing power of the mind and are more thoroughly described in my previous books.

HEALING POWER OF A WHEEL OF FORTUNE

The ability to image is vital to all human progress. Just as all reforms and advances in civilization began with the imagination, so all improvement in your life begins with improved mental pictures.

There is an ancient saying, "If you look up, you will always be provided for." It applies to your health, as well as to your wealth and happiness.

The German poet, Goethe, said: "What you can do or dream you can do, begin it. Boldness has genius, power and magic in it." Thus, if you desire something very much that seems completely out of reach, that is the time to deliberately turn the current of your expectation from "I cannot have" to "I can have." Through making a wheel of fortune you can go from despair to hope, from failure to success, from disease to health.

There is nothing new about this method for producing wonderful changes in your body and in your life. It is an old occult healing method that has recently been rediscovered by metaphysicians and psychologists.

One of the first steps to improved health is to definitely picture it. Generalities do not heal; they lack substance. Vague hopes and indefinite goals are not convincing to the mind which controls the body; whereas, a clear cut picture of your goal motivates both mind and body into a healing action.

There is nothing magical about being able to get the things you visualize. It is a mental law. What man imagines he can do, that can he do. Through the work of the imagination, every thought becomes a form. In thinking, man accumulates a mass of ideas and with his imagination he makes them into forms.

A man can imagine that he has some evil condition in body or affairs, and through the imagination he can build it up until it manifests. Disease has been reflected into susceptible minds as people merely talked about the disease as an awful reality. Under the old form of religion, the imagination played an important part in bringing great disasters to people. The mental pictures of an unsaved soul being thrown into the boiling lake of brimstone and burning forever caused guilt complexes, nervous breakdowns, mental illness, and physical disease.

Fortunately, man can use the same power to make good appear on every side. Make your body perfect by seeing perfection in it. To image one's self as perfect fixes the idea of perfection in the invisible mind substance, and the mind forces at once begin the work of bringing forth perfection.

HOW TO MAKE A WHEEL OF FORTUNE

An engineer in my first prosperity class devised a practical method for training the imagination to produce healthy results. He designed a "wheel of fortune" which has fascinated and helped scores of people.

On a large piece of poster board, he drew a round circle that encompassed most of the space. In the center of this circle he placed a picture of some religious symbol, denoting the help of a Higher Power in realizing his desires. From this innermost part, he drew four lines to the circumference of the circle, dividing his wheel of fortune into four parts, which he labeled (1) *business*, (2) *family*, (3) *spiritual*, and (4) *social and recreational*. In each of these four parts he then placed pictures of the results he desired to achieve in those phases of his life. Many people make an entire wheel of fortune for only one phase of their lives, however, such as prosperity, health, love or happiness.

Here are suggestions for making a wheel of fortune:

First: Do not show your wheel of fortune to anyone. Do not discuss it. Be very quiet about what you are doing. When you tell other people what you are trying to demonstrate in your life, they often mentally disagree with you, and may even try to neutralize your demonstration. Do not try to convince anyone that this method works. Just quietly use it and get results. That will be convincing to those who are illumined enough to appreciate this age-old method.

Second: In making a wheel of fortune, use big, beautiful pieces of poster board in a color that pleases you. Do not use small, colorless, drab material as a background, unless you want small, colorless, drab results. You are picturing your life as you want it to be, so be careful. Do not limit your good by picturing limita-tions on your wheel of fortune. A college professor made a small, crowded, drab wheel of fortune for travel abroad. It worked! He then had a crowded, drab, unpleasant trip. From this experience he learned the literal power of the imagination and never again limited his good by making small wheels of fortune. So use big, beautiful, colorful poster boards if you want big, beautiful, colorful results.

If you are making a wheel of fortune for healing, be sure to use light, bright colors that quicken and please the subconscious mind, which controls so many of the functions of the body. The following colors are suggested according to ancient color symbology:

1. For a financial wheel of fortune, use green or gold poster board.

2. For a wheel of fortune on increased spiritual understanding, use yellow or white poster board, symbolizing the "white light of Spirit."

3. For a wheel of fortune on intellectual accomplishment, such as getting a college degree, writing a book, play, or for other mental accomplishments, use blue poster board.

4. For a wheel of fortune on health, energy, increased activity, use orange or bright yellow poster board.

5. For a wheel of fortune on love and marriage, and increased harmony in one's life, use pink or rose poster board. Also orange or another bright color, such as shocking pink, helps to arouse one's emotional nature to the possibilities of love and marriage.

Third: Also use colored pictures on your wheel of fortune rather than black and white ones, since the imagination responds much more quickly to color. Again, by using colored pictures, you can expect colorful, happy results much more quickly.

Fourth: Do not clutter your wheel of fortune with too many pictures, words or phrases, ideas or affirmations. Instead make several wheels for the various phases of your life. Do not crowd any of them, unless you want cluttered, crowded results, because your imagination literally takes you seriously.

Fifth: If you make a financial treasure map for more income, a better job, nicer home, travel, etc., be sure to put play money (unless you can spare real money) and financial figures on your wheel of fortune. A business woman recently made a financial wheel of fortune, placing real money on it. She put it in her closet and spent some time each day secretly concentrating upon it. Shortly, through a revival of her business affairs, she became independently wealthy.

If you just put "things" you want on your wheel of fortune, you may receive them, but with extended credit which can lead to indebtedness. By placing money or its equivalent on your wheel of fortune, it opens your mind to receive it in such a way that there will be no financial burden attached to your desired results. For this purpose it also helps to place large checks in various denominations made out to you on your map, since most of one's large financial demonstrations arrive in the form of checks.

Sixth: Be sure to place a spiritual symbol on your wheel of fortune — preferably a colored picture of Christ (available at any religious bookstore). The picture of Christ gives your wheel of fortune a spiritual basis and also a divine protection. If those things which you have pictured are not for your highest good, the Christ consciousness is your divine protection and will help bring right things to pass. The Christ on your wheel of fortune produces a spiritual element, a divine power for accomplishment that your wheel would not otherwise have. It lifts it above the mental realm into the spiritual realm. *The name "Christ" has power to mold substance and produce the best results.*

A picture of the Bible, a Bible promise or Scripture verse, or some other spiritual symbol should be used if the Christ picture is not. It is also good to spiritually dedicate your wheel of fortune to God saying, *"Father, this or something better. Thy will be done."* This gives it increased spiritual power to work for you, and also complete divine protection.

Seventh: Put a statement about receiving on your wheel of fortune. Through making a wheel of fortune, you are not reaching out in consciousness trying to force anything to you. Instead, you are merely opening your mind to receive what is already at hand. Affirm: "MY GOOD IS AT HAND AND I GRATEFULLY RECEIVE IT NOW!"

You do not make a wheel of fortune to get anything from God. He has already given you everything as a potential blessing. "It is your Father's good pleasure to give you the kingdom," (Luke 12:32) and it is your good pleasure to receive it! Making a wheel of fortune of your desired good opens your mind to that receiving.

Even after the results are obtained, it is usually not wise to say much about it. A woman who makes a wheel of fortune to get a husband, and gets him, should never tell him later. This might cause him to feel trapped. We do not have to work on other people to get our good. We only have to work on our own thinking. Then, those who are receptive respond.

Eighth: After making your wheel of fortune, daily

spend time quietly and privately concentrating upon it, studying, absorbing, and "mothering" the ideas on it into expression. Imaging creates, but concentration hastens that creation into manifestation.[5]

Love is the drawing, attracting power of the mind. If you have used the imaging law previously without attaining the desires hoped for, it may be because you did not "love" your imaged desires into expression. Love is the magnet that draws the substance of the universe and fills your image with life. *Loving your pictured desire is the secret of making it a visible result!*

Live with your wheel of fortune for a while every day. Quietly enjoy it. Do not try to reason out how your desire will come to pass, and do not try to mentally force it into visibility. Just picture it and mentally enjoy the picture. Do so in a happy, relaxed, grateful mood. This is loving concentration — the kind that gets results.

Ninth: Keep working with a wheel of fortune as long as it interests you. When you have lost interest in it and/or when even a few things on it have manifested, it often has done its work. Put it aside and look at it again later. You will probably discover that in the interval it has continued to work for you. When you lose interest in it, it is time to release it completely and make a new one.

Make a new wheel of fortune at least at the beginning of each New Year. Make them for each phase of your life — health, wealth and happiness. Make them for other peoples' health, wealth and happiness, rather than worrying about other people or trying to force your ideas on them. In this sense, your wheel of fortune becomes a "prayer wheel" such as the Buddhists of Tibet have used for centuries.

---

5. See chapter on Concentration in *Pray and Grow Rich*.

There are many people who think they have reached the point that they need never make wheels of fortune. They scoffingly say, "I am *too advanced* for that." Don't you believe it! When people get too advanced to picture the good, they usually get too advanced to experience healing or prosperity, too!

PICTURING SHORTENS THE
DISTANCE TO YOUR GOALS

You never outgrow the picturing power of the mind. It is with you from birth to death and you should stay busy using it constructively. You should constantly be picturing something better than the best of what you are now experiencing. Wheels of fortune are a spiritual, scientific, psychological and practical way of helping you do this.

The healing power of the imagination is all powerful because *to fix your eye on a certain goal shortens the distance to attaining it.* The vision hour precedes the vision power. Imagination is the power of conception and what you can conceive, you can achieve! The same power that enables you to image pain, guilt, and failure is constantly at hand to image freedom from pain and a sound body. The power of the imagination must express in one way or another, but always it is at work, constructively or destructively. *It will not be stopped from functioning!* Much mental illness began with negative images held in the mind. A reverse process can bring reversed results.

Your imaging faculty found at the pituitary gland between the eyes can carry you to the heights or to the depths. The disciple, Bartholomew, symbolizes imagination. Just as Jesus saw him under a fig tree, a long way off, before he was visible to the natural eye, so does your imaging power behold the good sometimes long before it manifests. Your imagination has the power to bring things together in the mind, to produce new conditions in the body, new circumstances, environments and associations in your world. So, regardless of what your present life is like, there is hope for increased health, wealth and happiness for you. Get busy immediately tapping that great and wonderful power of your imaging faculty. You'll be glad you did, as you affirm often: "I PICTURE ONLY THE BEST FOR MYSELF AND OTHERS. MY EYES ARE SINGLE TO THE GOOD AND MY WHOLE BODY IS FILLED WITH LIGHT."

Note: Also see "The Imaging Law of Healing" chapter in *The Dynamic Laws of Healing*; "The Imaging Law of Prosperity" in *The Dynamic Laws of Prosperity*; and the chapter, "Create Your Prosperity Mentally First, in Pictures," in *Open Your Mind to Prosperity*.

Your healing power of

UNDERSTANDING

— 8 —

It may seem incredible to you that you have a mind power called "understanding" and that it has healing power. Yet I have seen this mind power known as "understanding" heal people many times.

In my own life it proved so. The first 20 years were anything but healthy. From early childhood on, I ran the gamut of ill health from anemia, low blood pressure, underweight, hypertension, and all the usual childhood diseases, right on through to surgery at the age of 15 that was attended by frightening complications and from which it took months to recover.

I can still taste the various medications that were literally poured down my reluctant throat by a sweet mother, whose only desire was to ward off illness. I am still trying to forget the black stockings (that would never stay up), the ugly high-top shoes, and the scratchy woolen underwear that I was required to wear from early fall until late spring, as well as those hated horn-rimmed glasses that pinched my nose year in and out.

In spite of my various bouts with ill health, I must have had a strong constitution to have endured all the "cures"!

Finally, in my late teens, I learned of the power that one's thoughts and feelings have upon one's health. Fascinated by such a possibility, I decided to free myself of ill health, and began experimenting with this healing idea, hoping that increased understanding could produce that result.

During the second period of life, my health was excellent, though I worked long hard hours and "burned the midnight oil" preparing for two separate careers—first in the business world and later in the ministry—while at the same time rearing a lively son and passing through the emotional anguish of the death of loved ones.

In spite of all these challenges, in that second period I suffered only minor illnesses which occurred when I was either extremely fatigued or emotionally distraught. Of course, I did not hesitate to seek medical or chiropractic treatment when needed. Nevertheless, during recent decades, my health has been as different as day and night, compared with the earlier periods.

My own experience has proved to me that the mind power of understanding is worth developing because understanding has healing power!

WHERE UNDERSTANDING IS LOCATED

The mind power known as "understanding," which includes all forms of knowing described as knowledge, wisdom, awareness, perception is located in the front brain just above the eyes, in the area of the conscious mind. *The front brain is considered one of the most important organs of intelligence in man.*

There is a theory that man has five physical senses and two metaphysical senses—mental telepathy and intuition—and these two metaphysical senses develop more and more as man unfolds his mind power known as understanding.[1]

The mind power known as "understanding" occupies a nerve center in the front brain along with its twin mind power, the will (Figure 8-1). The mind powers of will and understanding are meant to work together, with the understanding leading the will, rather than vice versa.

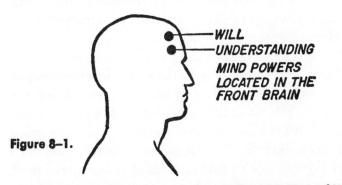

WILL
UNDERSTANDING
MIND POWERS
LOCATED IN THE
FRONT BRAIN

Figure 8–1.

Location of the Mind Powers of UNDERSTANDING and WILL.

The mind power of understanding is symbolized by Jesus' disciple, Thomas, who was called the doubter because he wanted to know about everything. The mind power of will is symbolized by Jesus' disciple, Matthew, the tax collector. The will is one of the executive powers of the mind that wishes to get things done in an outer way, often through hasty action, but can only wisely act when guided by intuitive understanding. Your twin mind powers of understanding and will are meant to

1. For developing one's telepathic and intuitive powers see chapters, "Your Genius Powers for Prosperity" and "Your Special Powers for Prosperity" in *The Dynamic Laws of Prosperity*.

work together from the front brain, with the understanding leading the will.

HOW INTUITIVE UNDERSTANDING HEALS

Understanding is natural to man. It expresses as intuitive knowing, which comes from the "still, small voice" within man, and often expresses through the perceiving power of the mind. You "see" with your understanding. You become enlightened through that intuitive knowing within you which often flashes to you as enlightenment.

A lady once came for counseling, insisting she had one problem, but as she talked, the thought telepathically flashed to me: "This lady is an alcoholic. That is her true problem. Only when that is healed, will her other problems resolve themselves." Six weeks later she confessed that alcoholism was the real problem, but she had been receiving spiritual treatment along that line all the time! With increased spiritual understanding came complete healing.

That inner light within you possesses the wisdom of the ages and when that enlightenment shines forth you say that you "see" what to do, meaning you "see" with your understanding. Seeing corresponds to understanding.

The ears and eyes are organs of the mind which correspond to man's understanding. *You do not see in your eyes so much as you see through them, according to what you understand.* The ear segregates sounds according to the mental choice of the inner mind, receiving what the mind mentally accepts, and refusing to hear anything else.

Health problems in the ears often indicate that a person is good and respectable in his own sight, but intolerant of those who do not think as he does. Ear trouble often indicates one who willfully wants his own way. He is letting his mind power of will rule his understanding, rather than vice versa. A mind attuned to the finer perceptions of its intuitive understanding, which dares to listen to and follow the guidance of the "still, small voice" of understanding from within, is constantly renewing, restoring the ears and eyes.

The mind power of understanding affects the whole body through the conscious mind. Through its intuitive flashes it becomes a channel through which energy of the Christ Mind at the crown of the head pours its superwisdom, first into the conscious mind in the front forehead, then into the great body brain in the solar plexus. As the seat of the subconscious activity of wisdom in the abdominal area of the body, the solar plexus is subconsciously affected by one's use of wisdom and understanding, which affects the stomach, heart and entire abdominal area of one's health.

YOUR FEET ARE CONNECTED WITH THE MIND POWER OF UNDERSTANDING

Also, the feet are especially sensitive to one's use of the mind power of understanding. In fact, the nerves of the feet are directly connected with the front brain and seat of understanding. There is an old saying, "The gait of a man is the fate of a man," meaning that one's interior nature is often reflected in the healthy or unhealthy state of one's feet. The whole man is affected by his feet because they are the base upon which he stands. *The feet are most sensitive to what is right or wrong and react accordingly.*

A woman who had been having an affair for years with a married man developed a mysterious disease in her legs and feet. Pain, swelling, and finally complete incapacity assailed her. The finest of doctors, including specialists at a famous clinic, were baffled. They could find no organic reason for her health problem. What they did not know is that the feet metaphysically symbolize understanding. When one refuses to live up to the highest and best he knows, baffling health problems in the area of the legs and feet are the natural result.

This woman, who was a Truth student and knew better, but who still refused to give up another woman's husband, continued to suffer from this baffling disease. She listened to her will rather than to her understanding. Even though she was warned by friends that her willfulness could cost her her life, she refused to listen. She could have had physical healing and emotional satisfaction in ways that were morally right if she would have affirmed: "ALL THINGS CONFORM TO THE RIGHT THING NOW, QUICKLY AND IN PEACE," and then would have dared to follow through by cleaning up her life.[2]

For healing poor circulation and cramps in the feet and legs, affirm often: "DIVINE UNDERSTANDING," and "LET THERE BE LIGHT."

---

2. Confusion concerning one's good in life can be cleared up and resolved by studying the chapter on the Divine Plan in *Open Your Mind to Prosperity.*

AFFIRMATIONS TO INCREASE HEALING
THROUGH UNDERSTANDING

Still another young woman was in need of healing of a severe case of rheumatism in the hands, arms, knees and feet, all of which were badly swollen and caused much pain. Seeking out a spiritual counselor, she was informed that there was no healing power in a bitter, unforgiving state of mind, and that she must transform her mind if she wished to transform her body. To cleanse her mind she decreed: "THE FORGIVING LOVE OF JESUS CHRIST HAS SET ME FREE FROM THE PAST, AND FROM THE RESULTS OF MISTAKES OF THE PAST. THERE IS NO CONDEMNATION IN CHRIST JESUS AND THERE IS NO CONDEMNATION IN ME."

To increase her understanding she declared: "I AM UPLIFTED AND UPHELD BY THE CHRIST MIND. NO DISEASE CAN EXIST IN THE CHRIST MIND AND NO DISEASE CAN EXIST IN ME. CHRIST IN ME NOW FREES, CLEANSES, AND HEALS ME."

This treatment in enlightenment went on day after day for two months until a complete healing had appeared.

The conscious use of understanding as it operates from the front brain affects the entire body, especially the ears, eyes and other of the five senses in the area of the head; the solar plexus region in the abdominal area; and the legs and feet.

THE POWER OF LIGHT TO HEAL

You release your mind power of understanding to heal when you affirm "light," because enlightenment is understanding in expression. As the sixteenth century physician Paracelsus explained: "Everything that lives, lives in light; everything that has an existence, radiates light. All things derive their life from light, and this light, in its root, is life itself. . . . By intuition, we are brought into contact with the *inner light*."

When your mind power of understanding expresses as light, it has a tremendous healing power. *The realization of light is essential to the handling of false growths that are considered malignant or cancerous.* Radium and various electrical rays, which have been widely used, symbolize the inner light or healing light of the Christ or All Knowing Mind. Scientists tell us that at the center of every atom in man's being is light. In diseased areas, this light seems to have gone out. When you use your mind power of understanding again to picture light in that part of the body, you release a healing power.

Dark emotions obscure this light. Thoughts of injustice and self-pity, as well as frightened thoughts of disease and death, cover up the light within each cell. Children and babies are usually considered immune to cancer because they are not yet filled with dark emotions which darken the cells, causing disease. Cancer is a disease that usually comes later in life after dark, troubled, devitalizing thoughts of uncertainty, fear, unforgiveness, discouragement, discontent and rebellion have been allowed to permeate the mind and body of man.

Spiritual enlightenment makes the body translucent. As the mind is filled with light, so is the body. Dead cells are cast off, and tempers, pettiness, emotional instability, jealousy, criticism, envy and animosity begin to dissolve through enlightenment.

X-rays reveal there is much difference between the bodies of human beings. X-rays of the hearts of two young men once appeared as a dark object in the chest of each with a slight pulsating movement. But the heart of one was much clearer on the X-ray than that of the other. Investigation revealed the "clear-hearted" one to be a Truth student who was constantly seeking greater understanding, while the other person was living an ordinary life of the world. It is little wonder that Solomon advised: "Wisdom is the principal thing; therefore get wisdom; Yea, with all thy getting, get understanding. . . Take fast hold of instruction; let her not go. Keep her, for she is thy life." (Proverbs 4:7,13)

HOW TO USE LIGHT FOR HEALING

A good healing treatment for dark, diseased parts of the body is to affirm: "LIGHT, LIGHT, LIGHT. LET THERE BE LIGHT. THE HEALING LIGHT OF THE CHRIST MIND PENETRATES AND BANISHES ALL DARKNESS FROM MY MIND AND BODY. I AM THE LIGHT OF MY WORLD."

A minister, along with several members of his congregation, witnessed a healing as they stood by the hospital bedside of a beloved member who was fighting for her life. Together they affirmed: "YOU ARE A CHILD OF THE LIGHT AND YOU WALK IN THE LIGHT." Their realization of light was the turning point in her healing.

"I CLOTHE MYSELF SAFELY ROUND WITH THE PURE WHITE LIGHT OF THE CHRIST, INTO WHICH NOTHING NEGATIVE CAN PENETRATE, AND OUT OF WHICH ONLY GOOD CAN COME," is a prayer which has healed countless people.

To meditate often on the statement, "I AM THE LIGHT OF MY WORLD," can flood your whole being with light and dissolve all darkness. *Light cannot injure light. Light is injured by nothing. It heals all. In the midst of this thought of light, you realize that you are immune from injury; that no one ever injured you. You forgive and forget any appearance of injury, now realizing it was an opportunity to prove the Truth.*

YOU HAVE THE WISDOM OF SOLOMON

Expressing your intuiton is the highest form of understanding. Solomon was considered a man of great wisdom and understanding because he dared to follow his intuitive knowing. The word "intuition" means "inner teacher." When you follow that still, small voice of intuitive knowing within, you are following the highest form of wisdom, and it will always lead you into paths of greater good. You, too, have the wisdom of Solomon! It is one of your mind powers.

HEALINGS THAT OCCURRED THROUGH USING INTUITIVE UNDERSTANDING

A lady who had suffered much, both physically and emotionally, feared the probable "incurable" diagnosis that her doctor might render if he examined her. Knowing of the healing power that comes from renewing the mind with increased understanding, this lady felt intuitively guided to go away for a few months to a spiritual retreat. She told no one of her alarming health problems. During the first month of her retreat, the health problems continued and she remained in much pain.

But, gradually, as she daily attended prayer services, spiritual lectures and talked with other people who had gained healings through spiritually retreating and expanding their understanding, her mind calmed and a great peace descended upon her. Another month in retreat passed and then she realized one day that all pain had left her, though she knew not when. *Renewal of the mind had brought renewal of the body.*

After spitting up blood for a long time, a businessman fearfully sought a physical examination, which revealed he had a form of tuberculosis considered incurable. His doctor informed him that through the use of certain drugs his condition could be arrested, but not cured. A slow death was inevitable.

This businessman realized that only increased understanding could save his life. He surprised his doctor by refusing the prescribed drugs for his condition, saying, "I intuitively know what to do. I am going away into the desert. There I shall go on a fast for 30 days and live in communion with God. I will get well."

His doctor replied, "If you go on a fast, as weak as you are, you will surely die!"

"I shall not die. I shall live, and in good health — not in a condition of arrested illness."

The next day this man left for the desert. There he found a suitable place to live and went on a fast. Day by day he began to feel better. Within 30 days he "knew" he had been healed. Returning to the city and to his job, he felt better than ever. After having fasted for 30 days, he found he no longer desired many foods that were not good for his health. An inner wisdom seemed to give him knowledge about many things. He was able to work harder than ever before, and even seemed to grow younger after this healing experience. One day on the street he met his doctor who looked at him and gasped, "I thought you were dead!"

When friends asked his secret, his reply was, "Prayer,

fasting and living in harmony with God and man. This gives increased understanding, which leads to every other blessing."

As Solomon wrote, "Happy is the man that findeth wisdom, and the man that getteth understanding. . . . She is a tree of life to them that lay hold upon her. And happy is every one that retaineth her." (Proverbs 3:13,18)

A Protestant minister had many problems, including that of a serious heart condition. A friend gave him a copy of my book, *The Dynamic Laws of Prosperity*. Upon reading it, he decided to apply the mental and spiritual laws described, and began by arising every morning at 5:30 for an hour of prayer, study and meditation. In this way he began developing his understanding in a much greater degree than ever before.

Within a year his financial income had gone from $6,000 to $30,000 as he took on certain fund-raising jobs for his denomination. When he appeared for a periodic check-up, the doctor found that his previously serious heart condition had faded completely. The physician exclaimed, "I wouldn't believe it if I had not taken both the previous and present X-rays personally. It's incredible, but your X-rays are clear. You have been healed." *Increased understanding had brought increased health and income to this minister.*

A veteran of World War II was required to enter a Veterans' Hospital again and again for a condition of tuberculosis, which seemed to come and go. Every type of appropriate drug had been used to promote healing, but nothing worked until he joined a prayer group formed by one of the volunteer workers at the hospital.

Through the increased understanding that resulted from prayer and study of inspirational literature, he

began to feel better. Later he was asked to join a group
of patients who were receiving experimental treatment
from still another special new drug. This time, the treatment worked, and this man was soon released from the
hospital. But the turning point had come, *only after he
had increased his understanding.*

THE PEACEFUL STATE OF MIND HEALED HIM

*Your mind power of understanding located in the
front brain especially responds to peace. A peaceful state
of mind is a healing state of mind.*

A businessman who had smoked for years to the detriment of his health attended a religious lecture on
"peace." On his way home, he reached for a cigar and
suddenly discovered that the realization of peace
received at that lecture had dissolved all desire within
him to smoke. The habit had simply fallen away. There
was not a minute's nervous distress or emotional reaction, only a great sense of freedom and gratitude. This
man never smoked again. A realization of peace, which
is the highest form of understanding, had healed him.
A powerful affirmation which releases the healing consciousness of peace is: "THE PEACE OF JESUS CHRIST IS
POURED OUT UPON ME (THIS SITUATION, DIAGNOSIS, PER-
SONALITY) AND I AM (IT IS) HEALED."

HOW TO ATTAIN YOUR GOOD MORE QUICKLY

*Through tapping and releasing the mind power of
understanding, located in the front brain, man ac-
complishes quickly that which under the slow action of*

human personality would take eons to achieve.
Understanding is supreme knowing. All the bitter lessons
that come through blundering ignorance can be avoided
when you decree that you are under the influence of
divine understanding.

You can get under the influence of such understanding, and begin releasing it from within out, when you affirm "divine intelligence." Dr. Emmet Fox explains in his
booklet, *The Seven Main Aspects of God.*[3]

"You should treat yourself for wisdom and intelligence
at least two or three times a week, by thinking about intelligence and claiming it for yourself.

"This practice will make every activity of your life
more efficient. There are sure to be some things you
could do in a better way than you are doing them.
Decreeing intelligence will bring such things to your
notice. If you are wasting time in certain directions,
decreeing wisdom will make the fact clear to you and you
will be shown a better way of working.

"When things in your life seem to be going wrong,
treat yourself for intelligence. When business or other
conditions appear to have reached a deadlock, treat
yourself for intelligence. When you seem to be up against
a stone wall and apparently there is no way out, treat
yourself for intelligence.

"If you have to deal with someone who is seemingly
very stupid or foolish, realize that divine intelligence
works in him because he is a child of God. If you get sufficient realization of divine intelligence, he will change
for the better. . . . The intelligence aspect is very important in its relation to the health of the body too."

---

3. Emmet Fox, *The Seven Main Aspects of God* (Marina del
Rey, CA: DeVorss & Co., 1970).

HOW TO DEVELOP THE VAST
BENEFITS OF WISDOM

When you affirm intelligence and understanding, you tap that inner knowing known as intuitive understanding, the highest form of wisdom. Intuitive knowing then appears as a flow of thought, a flash of inspiration, a hunch or idea that rushes into your mind and persists in getting your attention.

Remember this about intuitive knowing: It will always lead you into greater good provided you follow it quietly and nonresistantly, rather than questioning it, trying to reason it through, or talking to others about it.

The magic path of intuitive wisdom doesn't reason with you. It just points the way with its hunches and leaves you free to take them or leave them. If you follow through on your intuitive leadings, quietly, without arguing or reasoning, then you are on the magic path to your good. As Solomon promised, the man who dares to follow his intuitive understanding can have a long life, riches, honor, pleasantness, peace of mind, health and happiness. (Proverbs 3)

But if you stop to reason through or talk about your intuitive leadings to other people, trying to get their opinion, consent or approval, you will become confused and lose the guidance that came.

Nearly everyone has at some time touched this hidden wisdom as intuitive knowing or original inspiration, and has been astonished at its revelations. It helps you get to the truth of any matter quickly. When you first discover this flow of thought that seems independent of the reasoning mind, you may be puzzled as to its origin. But as you give attention to this faint whispering, it becomes stronger and you realize that it does not originate in the skull.

How do you develop it? You may "know" by simply affirming that you know all you need to know about any situation or personality that confronts you. "I AM SHOWN EXACTLY WHAT TO DO UNDER ALL CIRCUMSTANCES AND IN ALL PLACES. I KNOW WHAT I NEED TO KNOW WHEN I NEED TO KNOW IT. I AM ABLE TO DO EVERYTHING PERFECTLY NOW." Also, "I AM ALWAYS EXPRESSING WISDOM AND UNDERSTANDING. I MAKE RIGHT DECISIONS QUICKLY." So often we do not know because we say we don't know. Reverse the thought. Begin to say that you know what to do, and you will!

When you get an intuitive hunch to do or not to do something, follow through on it quietly and quickly. Henry Ford was past middle age when the idea intuitively came to him for the Ford car. He had a hard time raising the money to finance his experiments for building it. His friends thought Ford's ideas were ridiculous. His father wailed, "Henry, why did you give up a good $25 a week job in order to chase a crazy idea?" But Henry Ford intuitively dared to "chase a crazy idea" and you know the happy results.

Dr. Alexis Carrel, the famed scientist and doctor, once said that men of genius are simply men who have dared to listen to their intuition. But like Henry Ford, if you want to develop your intuitive understanding, you must be independent of the opinions of others.

The more you study the power of thought, the more careful you will become of your words; you will talk less and think more. How often we have talked away our good! Gibran in *The Prophet* has explained: "You talk when you cease to be at peace with your thoughts

. . . And in much of your talking, thinking is half-murdered."[4]

Sometimes people say, "But I do not seem very intuitive. How can I develop that which I don't seem to have?"

Everyone has intuitive wisdom within him. Usually those people who say they do not have it are simply the ones who haven't gotten quiet enough long enough to hear its leadings. If they would stop talking so much and listen more, the still, small voice of intuitive understanding would come alive in them, too.[5]

INTUITIVE UNDERSTANDING
COMES ALIVE IN QUIETNESS

That is why a daily period of prayer, meditation and inspirational reading is so powerful, refreshing and informative!

An engineer, who holds an executive position for one of America's leading industries once told me that he solved all his engineering problems through intuition. When any problem arose on the job that he did not know how to handle, he would retire to his office, sit *quietly* and wait for an idea or lead. Always he was shown how to proceed. He has gone from success to

---

4. Reprinted from *The Prophet* by Kahlil Gibran, with permission of the publisher, Alfred A. Knopf, Inc., New York. Copyright 1923 by Kahlil Gibran; renewal copyright 1951 by Administrators C.T.A. of Kahlil Gibran Estate and Mary G. Gibran.

5. See the chapter on the Wisdom Concept in *Open Your Mind to Prosperity*.

greater success through listening to and following his intuition.

Most of the great minds down through the ages became great through daring to follow the leadings of the inner voice within them. When asked what had been his secret for developing his famous theory of relativity, Albert Einstein replied, "The really valuable factor was intuition."

Intuition is a form of *cosmic knowing*. To live intuitively is to live fourth-dimensionally, one of the greatest gifts in living. As you affirm divine wisdom, understanding, intelligence, intuition, the seat of understanding in your front brain is stimulated and makes contact with the realm of super-intelligence in the Christ Mind at the crown of the head. Since this area has contact with universal knowledge, you penetrate the wisdom of the ages.

CASES OF MENTAL ILLNESSES HEALED
THROUGH INTUITIVE UNDERSTANDING

It pays to pray for other peoples' intuitive understanding, particularly if they are having mental health problems. A father whose only son was kleptomaniac (a thief), turned from shame, chagrin, fear of what his son might do, and painful watchfulness over him, to the practice of prayer. He asked God to illumine his own mind to give him understanding and wisdom concerning his boy.

As he was telling God all about his boy's mental trouble, his ungovernable disposition, his habit of taking things, it came to him very clearly that he was wasting the substance of his prayer in labeling his son the very thing he did not want him to be. This father stopped, astonished at the feeling of power and freedom that swept over him with his intuitive realization, and he prayed, "GOD BLESS MY BOY'S MIND AND MY MIND, TOO, AND HELP US TO THINK STRAIGHT, CLEAR, AND TRUE."

As he took the detectives off his boy's trail, and even talked over business matters with him, he found a wonderfully intelligent streak running through the lad's thoughts. Father and son were finally united in the intelligence of intuitive understanding, and the false mental state gradually disappeared.

An irate wife went to a spiritual counselor and began a tirade about her husband's cruelty, saying that he thought the meanest things, had the most suspicious mind, and used the most obscene language. She said that unless spiritual methods worked right away, she would leave him.

Quietly the counselor wrote on the back of an appointment card, "GOD HAS BLESSED YOUR MIND WITH LIGHT, LOVE AND INTUITIVE UNDERSTANDING. THROUGH YOUR MIND HE NOW BLESSES THE MIND OF YOUR HUSBAND WITH LIGHT, LOVE AND INTUITIVE UNDERSTANDING." She asked the woman to rest quietly and repeat the words: "GOD HAS BLESSED MY MIND AND THE MIND OF MY HUSBAND WITH LIGHT, LOVE AND INTUITIVE UNDERSTANDING."

When the counselor returned a few minutes later, the woman was gone. Several months afterward she returned, bringing her husband with her. Laughingly she remarked, "My husband says he never saw such a change in a woman, and I know it is because God has blessed our minds, hearts and home with light, love and intuitive understanding."

If there were a record of all the names of persons who have been released from mental institutions, healed of cerebral diseases, freed from distorted mental states, renewed in mind and restored to perfect sanity, hundreds of people—who have never realized what their own intuitive thoughts and prayers could accomplish for others—would be astonished!

Instead of condemning a person, calling him a fool, imbecile, crazy or insane, declare instead: "GOD HAS BLESSED YOUR MIND WITH LIGHT, LOVE, WISDOM AND INTUITIVE UNDERSTANDING. YOU KNOW WHAT TO THINK, SAY AND DO AT ALL TIMES AND IN ALL PLACES. YOU EXPRESS YOUR INTUITIVE UNDERSTANDING PERFECTLY NOW."

UNDERSTANDING HAS A SOLUTION
FOR EVERY PROBLEM

A new flood of life comes to those who open their minds and bodies to understanding. It raises the atomic vibration of the organism above the usual disintegrating thought currents of the earth.

The ebb and flow of understanding produces a fine essence of life, which flows through the nerves, and also courses through the blood. Your increased understanding also affects the great ganglia (nerve centers) of the sympathetic system, regulating the functions of respiration, circulation and digestion, as well as the lesser nerve centers near the heart and stomach. This nervous system makes you feel more joyous and healthy as you develop you mind power of understanding. The cerebro-spinal system consisting of the brain and spinal cord, with branches to various parts of the body which give one the power to move, also respond to your increased understanding.

The development of your mind power of understanding is one of the most advanced metaphysical developments you can make! You can heal your body and

revolutionize your life through increased understanding.
Once you have learned to harness and use your intuitive
understanding, you will not go back to the old trial and
error method of reason, logic, will-power, any more than
one who has learned the advantages of harnessing and
using electricity would go back to coal, oil and the old
ways of living. Intuitive understanding has a beautiful
solution for any dilemma.

For this purpose center your attention in the front
forehead and quietly relax into the thought, "BE STILL
AND KNOW THAT I AM GOD. I AM THE LIGHT OF MY WORLD."
Think of the light then permeating and penetrating your
entire body and all your affairs. In that light is increased
energy, guidance and healing power.

From the top of your head to the tip of your toes,
sweep your body with the thought of light and enlighten-
ment. Then follow through on the intuitive understand-
ing that comes as you affirm often: "I AM INTUITIVE
UNDERSTANDING. WITHIN ME IS THE WISDOM OF THE AGES.
THE MIND THAT KNOWS HOW IS SHOWING ME NOW. THE
MIND THAT KNOWS WHERE IS LEADING ME THERE. THE MIND
THAT KNOWS WHEN WILL TELL ME THEN."

Your healing power of

WILL

— 9 —

A spiritual counselor was called to the home of a young child who was in a coma and so weak that her pulse could hardly be detected.[1] Several physicians who had been called in decided she had a brain tumor and that an operation was her only hope of survival. In her weakened condition, her mother felt an operation might be fatal and had sent for the spiritual counselor.

This spiritual counselor insisted upon knowing the events that had led up to this sudden illness. The facts were these:

A few days previously the little girl had come running to her mother, breathless, jubilant, excited because some of her friends were giving a party and had invited her.

But her mother said sharply, "You are not going."

---

1. H.B. Jeffery, *The Principles of Healing* (Ft. Worth, Texas: Christ Truth League, 1939).

"I have to go," pleaded the child. "I said I would. I promised. They are expecting me."

"You cannot go!"

"I am going!"

"You are not. I am your mother, and I say you're not going—and you aren't."

Lamely the child asked, "Why not?"

"Never mind why. You cannot go."

This little girl kept on insisting until she had worked herself up into a tantrum, throwing herself on the floor kicking and screaming. But the mother kept on saying, "No!" *Since the mother's will was stronger, the child was mentally beaten into insensibility.*

Later it was revealed that there was no tumor. The trouble was purely emotional. Physically, there had been a violent contraction of the spinal muscles between the shoulders. The muscles that were related to the upper spine had spasmed, and this had temporarily interfered with the circulation of the blood to the brain. The child had been thrown into this state by the tension of wills clashing. There had been warfare on the mental battlefield and the child, in her natural resistance to an unexplained harness of will, became paralyzed by the tension of her mind.

Through spoken inspiring words, which relaxed the will, the child was restored to health.

THE LOCATION OF THE WILL

There is an ancient metaphysical teaching, "The will is the man." The will is the focal point around which all mind action centers when the mind is harmonious. Schools of philosophy from ancient times have taught that the will and understanding are mind powers closely related. When man's will is working strongly, he corrugates his brow and his quick understanding causes his eyes to "flash."

The closely related mind powers known as "understanding" and "will" should be deliberately activated in one who wishes to regain his health. These faculties have the power to make connection with the previously obscured vitality within the organism.

The idea of energy has often been associated with willpower. Your mind power of will is located in the forehead in the front brain, just above the mind power of understanding. Its location is significant (see Figure 9-1). The understanding and will are twin mind powers, meant to work together, with the understanding leading the will, though usually it has been the other way.

The will usually tries to coerce man's intuitive understanding into doing that which the will wants done quickly and forcefully, rather than vice versa. The will is supposed to listen to and follow man's quiet intuitive leadings.

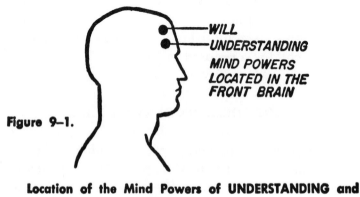

Figure 9–1.

Location of the Mind Powers of UNDERSTANDING and WILL.

Usually when you have had intuitive guidance come to you—when you have had those quick flashes of inner knowing—your will has rarely wanted to follow that guidance. Instead your will, more often than not, tried to argue you down. It probably tried to force its own logical reasoning in the matter quickly.

If you listened to your will, with all of its logical reasonings which it wished expedited quickly, and did not follow your intuitive understanding, you became confused and made costly mistakes. Later you realized that your intuition was right all the time and that you should have followed its quiet wisdom, rather than listening to your loud, clamoring, forceful human will, whose logical arguments came to naught.

There is a warning that describes willful people: "Hurry, worry, *bury*."

NOTHING WRONG WITH WILL

Not that there is anything wrong with the will. Your will is wonderful. It is your lifeline as found in popular statements, such as, "He lost the will to live." "He lost the will to win." As for the power of the will on the body, the eighteenth-century German philosopher, Arthur Schopenhauer, well known for his metaphysical doctrine of the will, once explained: "My body is the objectification of my will. The will is my real self. The body is the expression of the will."

Your will is all important. It is quite necessary for your health, wealth and happiness. But that will must know its place. It must be tempered with intuitive understanding. Your will must be taught to follow your intuitive leadings, rather than fight them. It is then that you truly have "the will that wins."

When man's intuitive understanding is activated, becoming spiritually illumined, and when the will has been trained to follow the leadings of intuition, man is then able to place his will in line with the universal will. Then, all the promises of God automatically become a part of his life!

Understanding is an inner realization, but it is through the will that everything realized within is expressed and manifested as happy results in one's outer life. It is through the understanding that the will is educated and trained. The two must work together harmoniously for perfect soul development, as well as for perfect physical and mental health. If the will acts without the understanding, chaos results in one's mind, body and affairs.

The will, working alone in a headstrong way without the benefit of the twin mind power of intuitive understanding, has built many health problems into the mind and body of man through the subconscious mind. These health problems can be dissolved when the will begins to join forces with intuitive understanding.

HEALTH PROBLEMS CAUSED BY WILLFULNESS

When the will is permitted to act on its own, man becomes emotional and willful. These states of mind lead to all kinds of bodily discord. Willfulness makes tenseness, and a tense mind ties knots in the nerves, muscles and tendons of the whole organism. Willful people often complain of a feeling like that produced by a tight band around the head. This feeling results from the pressure of the thought which the mind power of will

located in the front brain has laid hold of and is cling-
ing to in that area of the body.

*Every organ of the body is affected by the action of the
will.* When this mind power becomes fixed in certain attitudes, it holds the whole body to those fixed attitudes,
as though the body were held in a vice. *Crystallized,
fixed states of mind cause crystallized, fixed health problems in the body.*

The solar plexus in the abdominal region of the body
is a brain and nerve center. This solar plexus area directs
the circulation, digestion, and assimilation. Through
this plexus area the ruling thoughts of the head, working through the mind power of will, are carried into the
body.

Hard, dictatorial, willful states of mind will harden
the heart. These forceful states of mind act through the
solar plexus and bring limitation upon the whole body.
Hardened arteries are too often the result of *hard*, willful
thoughts. *We do not need less will. We only need more
understanding of how to direct it.*

Stubborn, willful, resistant, fighting states of mind
congest the life flow, and are often followed by cramps
and congestion.

The will often compels the use of various organs
beyond their normal capacity; strained nerves and muscles, impaired sight and hearing result. Deaf people
should be treated for freedom from stubbornness.

The determination to have one's own way, regardless
of the rights of others, tends to stop the free action of the
heart. The stomach is then sympathetically affected.
People with such health problems seldom realize that it
is their own set determination that is destroying their
health. They are sometimes slow in accepting the intuitive understanding that is necessary for the untangling
of mistakes made by an arrogant will.

An exaggerated idea of their self-importance has blinded their will and deafened it to its twin power of intuitive understanding. People who are willfully contentious of their personal rights place themselves in mental, emotional and physical bondage and stop their spiritual growth. Often, their egos have to be crucified before they are willing to begin working with intuitive understanding again, which is their only hope of healing.

MARITAL DISCORD CAUSED BY WILLFULNESS

Once upon a time there was a husband and wife who couldn't get along. Each one tried to force the other to do what he wished. Neither would give the other any emotional freedom. Of course, they both had serious health problems.

The husband was losing his eyesight and hearing. He wore thick-lensed glasses, yet could hardly see. After several operations on his eyes, he still stumbled around. He also wore the most expensive hearing aid available, but could barely hear. After their innumerable quarrels, this man often had heart attacks and usually retreated to the hospital to recuperate, where he made a nice recovery free from his wife's endless nagging.

As for his vastly overweight wife, she suffered from a diabetic condition, heart and stomach trouble. Neither she nor her husband could have a normal conversation without relating all the faults of the other. Once the wife telephoned me, "You are one of the few people my husband will listen to. The next time he comes to church, I want you to tell him to do this—and—that, etc."

Her husband finally found a way of avoiding his wife's constant demands. When she tried to tell him what to do, he would turn off his hearing aid!

The same willfulness that made this couple sick also kept them bound to each other. Each vowed he was waiting for the other to die, in order to gain complete control of their combined wealth. *Willfulness locked them in a vice of ill health.*

HOW TO TREAT WILLFULNESS

In her book *Beyond Ourselves*[2] Catherine Marshall describes the necessity for getting free of such willfulness as "ego-slaying." She explains how necessary it is to our spiritual and mental health. Ego-slaying is also a "must" for physical well-being.

For all willfulness, the healing treatment should contain affirmations of spiritual understanding. *The will is not to be broken, but disciplined and directed. The will can be strengthened by being constantly linked with understanding. Intuitive understanding quickens and makes it alive.*

Instead of saying "I don't know," "I do not understand," declare "I am one with intuitive understanding. I know what to do and I do it."

You may know by simply affirming that you know. This is not willful egotism, but a spiritual knowing you are invoking. Then do not act until you get an inner, intuitive assurance. That assurance is an indication that you have direct fusion with the Mind of God or the realm of Divine Intelligence. It pours forth through the crown of the head into your mind powers of understanding and will in the front forehead, through them into the solar plexus region, and then throughout the entire body. A

---

2. Catherine Marshall, *Beyond Ourselves* (Carmel, N.Y.: Guideposts, Inc., 1961).

general quickening of both mind and body then takes place.

In observing willfulness in others, it is wise to treat for relaxation of the will and for a general letting go of the whole system. The universal healing treatment for willfulness as given by Jesus was, "Not my will but Thine be done." (Luke 22:42) This emotional surrender causes personal will to let go and a unification of man's limited will with God's universal good will can then take place. When this is accomplished, a healing occurs in both mind and body.

You can treat metaphysically against personal willfulness as you declare: "I RELAX, LOOSE, LET GO AND LET GOD. I LET GO AND GROW. I LET GO AND TRUST." And, you can treat others by declaring these ideas for them, too.

WILLFULNESS IS MENTAL MURDER

As a product of the natural man, will is often a destructive force. Nearly all our systems of training children have been based on breaking the will in order to gain authority over the child and obedience from him.

The right to exercise freedom of will was given to man in the beginning. *The will is not to be broken but directed by intuitive understanding.* Jesus, the Christ, was not negative in the use of any of His mind powers. He did not teach a doctrine of submission. Instead He claimed for Himself and His followers divine power and authority in the use of their mind powers.

Never try to change or break another's will for that is mental murder. The force of human will usually generates rebellion and conflict. When a person tries to use his human will to force someone else to do what he personally wants, his willfulness reacts upon himself, not only as mental confusion and emotional upsets, but also as bad health.

A father had a son that he had gotten along with reasonably well until the son became a teenager. As this teenager began to develop more as an adult, the father tried to continue forcing him to be a child. In a rage one day the father stormed, "I am going to break his will, if necessary."

Trying to break the son's will proved to be mental murder, but for the father. The boy was somehow able to throw off the inharmony. But the father developed heart trouble and other health problems. He died one day after another fit of willfulness. *Never try to break another's will, for that is mental murder, and the mental murder you commit may be your own!*

WILLFULNESS BROUGHT CONFUSION AND MENTAL ILLNESS

It is not right for a person to submit his will to the control of another personality. We should be careful not to enter into any healing system that interferes with freedom. Any system that suppresses the will is radically wrong. It is the work of the true spiritual healer to instruct, showing cause and remedy from a *spiritual* viewpoint. *All other methods are temporary.*

A man may have a paralyzed arm through selfish desire for money, and though he may find temporary relief in mere mental suggestions of health, he will never get permanent healing until he understands the prospering laws governing substance and conforms to them willingly.

If you believe that you are under the control of another's will, your own will is gradually weakened and you can even lose control over it. The will must be strengthened by being constantly united with understanding. Whereas mental force weakens the will, spiritual understanding quickens and makes it alive.

A young woman who had a very strong will which she had not learned to balance with understanding, learned of the power of thought and became fascinated by it. She decided to use her mind power to begin making other people do what she wished them to do.

Although she had a fine husband and several nice children, she decided she wanted an attractive businessman who was unmarried. She persisted in trying to use mental force to attract him, as she affirmed that he would ask her to marry him.

When she tried mentally to will it, this man's only reaction was one of repulsion. In turn, the willfulness which she tried to send out to him, only reacted upon herself.

She became mentally confused and emotionally upset. Finally she divorced her husband, still determined to marry the other man, but it did not work. The more she tried mentally to will this result, the more confused she became. Finally she had to be committed to a mental hospital for treatment, while the man she had tried to attract happily married someone else. Her former husband also later remarried and gained custody of their children.

When a person tries to force his good to him, he always get hurt; he always suffers. Under some circumstances a person may temporarily force to him what he willfully desires, but it will not be satisfying. Remember, *"What you fight to get, you must fight to keep."*

CHOICE OF THE RIGHT KIND OF WILL

The accumulation of ignorance and its destructive re-sults on both mind and body can be dissolved through the spoken word.

Affirmations made in the head alone are followed by a feeling of tension, as if bands were drawn across the forehead. When this state of mind sinks into sub-consciousness, the nerves become tense. If the practice is continued, nervous tension results.

Developing the mind power of will in a positive way is not the work of an instant. The way is through daily relaxation,[3] meditation, prayer and spiritual study. Silently meditating upon the thought, "NOT MY WILL BUT THINE BE DONE," opens the will located in the front brain to the inflow of energy and power from the Christ Mind at the crown of the head. After this energy connects in the front brain, it then flows into the whole body.

The will plays a leading part in all systems of healing. The simple statement, "I WILL TO BE WELL WITH GOD'S HELP," gathers the forces of mind and body about the central idea of wholeness in the body.

Among the apostles of Jesus, Matthew represents the mind power of will, and Thomas represents the mind power of understanding. Matthew was the tax-gatherer who sat at the gate, representing the executive part of the government. Just so the will is the executive faculty of the mind and carries out the orders given it. All thoughts that go into or out of man's consciousness pass the gate of the conscious mind in which is seated the will. If the will understands its job, the character and value of every thought is inquired into and a certain tribute is exacted for the benefit of the whole man.

---

3. See chapter on Relaxation in *Pray and Grow Rich.*

The word "will" means "purpose, choice, determina-tion." *Whatever you choose, you are willing. All things can be done by choice. Make deliberate choice the great conscious action of your mind.* If you choose life and health, then you are willing yourself back to life and health. Your will for health is a powerful factor in bring-ing it forth. *The will is the master builder of the body.*

So many people ignorantly will for themselves just the opposite of what they want: ill health, financial limita-tions, and family problems. They will these things when they choose to think about them, talk about them, give their attention to them.

GOD'S WILL IS FOR YOUR GOOD HEALTH

Some cases of illness do not respond readily to the treatment, "NOT MY WILL BUT THINE BE DONE," because the belief has been erroneously fixed in the patient's mind that God wills suffering. But God's will for all His creation is only good. When the patient realizes this, then perfect harmony can be activated in his mind and body, and this is the perfect will of God.

Giving up the will of God is not a negative process. It simply makes way for one's deepest desires to take expres-sion. The will of God is the open door of fulfillment of all your dreams.

If God's will for you was not good health, you could not be healed no matter what you did! A famous doctor recently stated that patients who believe God's will for them is health show greater resistance to disease and much quicker recovery power, than patients who doubt this. Celebrated psychologist, Carl Jung, has stated, "I have treated many hundreds of patients, and there has not been one whose problem in the last resort was not that of finding a religious outlook on life."

When man links himself with the will of God, he develops superior executive ability. He swiftly brings forth mind power that under the slow action of human consciousness would take ages to develop. Development of these superior mind powers can then lead man to the fulfillment of his dreams.

In his book, *The Sermon on the Mount,*[4] Dr. Emmet Fox explains:

"A tragic mistake that is often made by orthodox religious people is to assume that the will of God for them is bound to be something very dull and uninviting, if not positively unpleasant. . . . The Truth is that the will of God for us always means greater freedom, greater self-expression, wider, newer, brighter experiences; better health, greater prosperity, wider opportunity of service to others, and a life more abundant.

"If you are ill or in poverty, or obliged to do work that you dislike; if you are lonely, or if you have to mix with people who displease you; you may be certain that you are not expressing the will of God, and as long as you are not expressing His will, it is natural for you to experience inharmony; it is equally true that when you do express His will, harmony will come.

"It is the will of God that we should all lead healthy, happy lives, full of joyous experiences; that we should develop freely and steadily, day by day and week by week, as our pathways unfold more and more unto the perfect day."

---

4. Emmet Fox, *Sermon on the Mount* (New York: Harper & Row, Publishers, Inc., 1934).

DARE TO CALL ON GOD'S WILL FOR YOU

Say to yourself often: "GOD'S WILL FOR ME IS SUPREME GOOD. GOD'S WILL FOR ME IS HEALTH, WEALTH AND HAPPINESS. I AM WILLING TO DO THE GOOD WILL OF GOD, WHICH IS THE OPEN DOOR TO FULFILLMENT OF ALL MY DREAMS. GOD'S GOOD WILL MANIFEST IN MY LIFE NOW."

When you dare to think in this way, you open the way to bring forth swiftly the good that otherwise would take ages to unfold in your life.

When you are tempted to try mentally to control other people, relax your will by decreeing: "I HAVE NO NECESSITY TO TRY TO CONTROL PEOPLE OR EVENTS. I RELAX AND RELEASE PEOPLE AND EVENTS TO THE PERFECT WILL OF GOD."

The will is not to be retarded but strengthened along all lines. Health of mind and body is produced by rounding out the mind power of will through joining it to understanding. For this purpose affirm often: "GOD WORKS IN ME TO WILL AND TO DO WHATSOEVER HE WISHES ME TO DO, AND GOD CANNOT FAIL. THEREFORE I CANNOT FAIL."

People have fearfully prayed, "If thou wilt, O Lord, bring this to pass," but often with no visible results. Instead use a definite, positive will-not-be-put-off attitude, a determined, "I WILL HAVE THY WILL DONE IN THIS MATTER NOW" attitude. This is a positive force that always brings the best results to pass.

There is a saying, *"What God wills, He also fulfills."*

ANOTHER'S WILL CAN CAUSE DISEASE FOR YOU

By affirming God's will in your life, you protect yourself from the willful, limited thoughts of other people. Such poisonous thoughts actually bring disease to receptive minds, which have not been taught how to protect themselves.

A businessman, upon learning of the power of the will to kill or cure, realized that for many years he had suffered from the common cold during the winter season, because other people willed it. He realized that he would "take a cold" because of the cold thoughts of other people directed toward him in the form of criticism and condemnation. He started mentally saying, "No, no, no" to all mental brick-bats thrown his way, and soon was free of colds that had plagued him for years.

You must learn to close the door of your mind to the negative willfulness of other people. Malignant thoughts can contribute to cancerous conditions. Sometimes these malignant thoughts are directed toward a person by someone else. There once was a dear little lady who was financially dependent upon her daughter. She always seemed pleasant, helpful, uncomplaining. Yet she suffered from cancer of the face.

Since there seemed nothing in her disposition to warrant such a malignant growth, her spiritual counselor searched further and discovered a son-in-law who constantly directed angry, vicious thoughts and words at this lady. He resented her presence in his home, which somewhat restricted the family group. Over a period of years, his malignant resentment of her presence was directed at the face of his mother-in-law. She had unconsciously accepted this malignant resentment, which had resulted in a malignant disease.

Incurable condemnation produces incurable disease. Such condemnation can be cleared up through using a series of statements such as these: "THERE IS NO CONDEMNATION IN CHRIST JESUS, AND THERE IS NO CONDEMNATION IN, THROUGH OR ROUNDABOUT ME. I FULLY AND FREELY FORGIVE. I LOOSE AND LET GO. I LET GO AND LET GOD. NOT

MAN'S WILL BUT GOD'S WILL IS DONE IN MY MIND, BODY AND
AFFAIRS NOW."

Disagreements, the clashing of opinions between two
or more people, and general willfulness can result in arthritis. This is one of the oldest diseases, found even in
the skeletons of dinosaurs. Aging people often develop
arthritis in proportion to their stiffened attitudes toward
others. Just as arthritis responds physically to heat, it responds metaphysically to warm thoughts and emotions,
such as these: "THERE IS NO CONFLICT IN GOD'S WILL OF
GOOD FOR HIS CHILDREN, AND THERE IS NO CONFLICT IN ME.
I LOOSE AND LET GO ALL OPPOSITION, CONTENTION , CON-
FLICT, OR STIFFNESS IN MY THOUGHTS, ACTIONS AND REAC-
TIONS TO MY FELLOWMAN."

*Many health problems are unconsciously resolved
when a person stops trying to control the lives of other
people.*

A prominent electrical engineer in England early in the
century decided to investigate spiritual healing, expecting
to expose it as a hoax. Instead, he got so fascinated with
the power of the mind to heal that he became a prominent mental healer.

Later he pointed out that people around a sick person can keep him sick by their own diseased thoughts.
He warned that relatives, friends, even the doctors and
nurses, could intensify the patient's disease, and that one
should be careful with whom he associated during illness. Fortunately, *through affirming God's will, you neutralize another's diseased pictures of you.*

YOUR "MUST" POWERS FOR HEALING

Your mind power of understanding is quiet and con-
templative in character. From it you learn what to do;

whereas, your mind power of will is your busy mental executive that carries through on the guidance received from your understanding. *Your will moves to action all the other faculties of your mind.*

These twin mind powers working together are your "must" powers for healing. You can activate and coordinate them to produce happy results for you as you affirm: "I RELAX AND LET GO. I RELAX AND LISTEN FOR THE VOICE OF INTUITIVE UNDERSTANDING TO UNFOLD ITS GOOD TO ME. I WILL TO DO THE GOOD WILL OF GOD JOYOUSLY. ONLY GOOD SHALL COME TO ME."

Your healing power of

ORDER

— 10 —

An unhappy, overweight woman had every problem: she could not get along with her family; she could not keep a job; she could not lose weight. Often she had attended prayer groups and had consulted with spiritual counselors, apparently to no avail.

One day when she was confined to her bed quite ill, she telephoned asking that a counselor come to her home to pray with her. Upon entering the house, the counselor suddenly understood why no one had previously been able to help this frustrated, sick woman: Her house was in a state of great disorder. Strewn all over were old newspapers, magazines, empty medicine bottles, clothes, household effects, debris of every kind.

At this point the frightened, sick woman might have wailed with Job: "My soul is weary of life . . . Before I go whence I shall not return, Even to the land of darkness and of the shadow of death; The land dark as midnight, The Land of the shadow of death, *without any order.*" (Job 10:1,21,22)

Upon viewing this state of wild disorder, it was easy for the counselor to understand why this woman had so many problems. She was violating the first law of the universe: ORDER. The counselor explained that just as order is Heaven's first law, order is also earth's first law, too. It was suggested that if this woman wanted to get her problems solved, she should begin by invoking the *healing power of order.*

Together they affirmed: "DIVINE ORDER IS NOW ESTABLISHED IN ME BY THE POWER OF THE INDWELLING CHRIST. DIVINE ORDER IS NOW ESTABLISHED IN MY MIND, BODY AND AFFAIRS BY THE POWER OF THE INDWELLING CHRIST. I AM IN DIVINE ORDER! MY MIND IS IN DIVINE ORDER. MY BODY IS IN DIVINE ORDER. MY AFFAIRS ARE IN DIVINE ORDER. MY RELATIONSHIPS ARE IN DIVINE ORDER. EVERY PHASE OF MY WORLD IS IN DIVINE ORDER. DIVINE ORDER HEALS, PROSPERS AND GUIDES ME NOW."

As this confused soul began to call on divine order, her mind cleared and her emotions calmed. She called in help and cleared out her house, throwing out all those precious old newspapers, magazines and empty medicine bottles she had cherished so long. As she affirmed, "I LET GO WORN-OUT THINGS AND WORN-OUT CONDITIONS. DIVINE ORDER IS NOW ESTABLISHED AND MAINTAINED IN ME AND IN MY WORLD," she began to feel better. Her family became easier to live with in a non-cluttered atmosphere. Like Hezekiah of old, when she set her house in order, instead of dying she lived. (II Kings 20) In due time she lost weight, got a job, and went on to a happier way of life, but only after she began to observe the healing law of order.

LOCATION OF THE ORDER CENTER IN THE BODY

Order is one of your 12 mind powers, located at a large nerve center just behind the navel in the solar plexus region of the body. Perhaps it comes as a surprise to learn that order is first a mind power. We have often thought of it as something we rushed about accomplishing in an outer way.

Ironically the word "inharmony" means "something is out of order." Inharmony in mind, body or affairs indicates a need for developing your mind power of order. Order begins *within*.

Of Jesus' apostles, James, son of Alphaeus, is symbolic of the mind power of order because his work was to cooperate with the other disciples. Order, from within, produces cooperation and the highest form of harmony.

There has always been divine order in the universe and there always will be. When things do not seem in divine order, remind yourself that the lack of order is not in the universe, but in your own attitudes and emotions which may have been reflected as lack of cooperation with others.

When things seem inharmonious and out of order, instead of rushing about frantically trying to make them right in an outer way; instead of trying to change other people and make them more orderly (this process usually leads only to more disorder); remind yourself that lack of order first exists *within* you. If you can get your own thoughts and feelings orderly, then the people, situations and even the universe about you will respond in a more orderly way.

When it dawns on you that you have the mind power of order within you, that you can call upon it to make all things right in your world, this realization takes away the tension, friction, or the need to push and force your good.

If more people realized the true location of order as a mind power within them which they can easily release, there would be fewer nervous breakdowns, heart attacks, or cases of hypertension. There would be a diminishing need for doctors, psychiatrists, or mental hospitals.

HOW YOUR ORDER CENTER FUNCTIONS

As you begin to call on and release your mind power of order, everything in your world will begin to respond. Some departments of your life will react more quickly than others, but if you will decree divine order, somehow it will work in every phase of your world. More and more you will see harmony and order begin to work quietly, harmoniously, thoroughly. You will realize the wisdom of Paul's advice to the Corinthians: "Let all things be done decently and in order." (I Corinthians 14:40)

Since the mind power of order is located at the navel (as shown in Figure 10-1) in the emotional, subconscious area of the body, this indicates that *order is first an emotional quality.* The ancient philosopher, Philolaos, felt

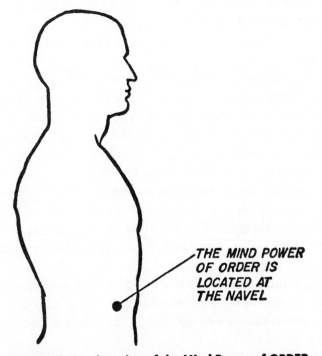

THE MIND POWER OF ORDER IS LOCATED AT THE NAVEL

Figure 10–1.   Location of the Mind Power of ORDER.

that the seat of emotions in the body was located at the navel, as did the famous Madame Blavatsky. Psychic seer and reincarnationist, Edgar Cayce, described this center of order at the navel as the "lyden gland," which was an ancient term.

Order works through emotional harmony. Order that is achieved without harmonious, emotional agreement is not order. It is conflict and leads not to order, but to confusion!

The "perfect homemaker" who makes all the members of her family miserable with her "orderliness" is a good example of outer order that leads only to confusion and inharmony, because there is no inner harmony or emotional agreement connected with her wishes. *Such supposedly orderly people often suffer from ill health and emotional problems of the worst kind, as well as contributing to the health problems of those about them because of their lack of understanding of what is truly orderly.*

Supposed order which is accomplished through inharmony defeats its purpose completely since something is out of order emotionally and in the atmosphere. *Outer order which is accomplished at the price of unpleasantness is not order at all. It is stringent willfulness. The unpleasantness and tension caused by it in either home or business atmosphere adds immeasurably to the ill health of those exposed to such an atmosphere.*

There is a quip: The way to begin your day at the office is to (1) Get organized; (2) Telephone your spouse; (3) Get organized again!

In relation to order, it is good to have a master plan for success, but there should be a relaxed flexibility expressed in executing that plan. This is divine order at its best.

One man's type of order leads to a thought-out system

of filing his papers; whereas another's provides him with a desk piled high with letters and papers. One keeps early hours; the other, late ones. They both do business, and are perhaps equally successful in their undertakings. Who is to judge their ways and pronounce judgment upon them? *Each of us must ascertain his own scheme of order in his possessions and in unfolding his life.*

THE WONDERFUL RESULTS OF DIVINE ORDER

Many physical ailments that people have in the stomach and abdominal region near the navel result from inharmony and lack of order in their emotions and lives. When they begin to affirm "divine order," that helps to begin putting their own thoughts and affairs in order. Often a healing comes quickly. If you have health problems, financial problems, family problems, or suffer from confusion and uncertainty, you can begin clearing them all away by affirming "divine order."

One person who knew she had the mind power of order within her which could be released through her decrees, used words of divine order to locate a lost key, to ease the pain in a hand burned from scalding water, to gain protection and peace of mind while traveling on ice-covered streets, to start a car when the battery was weak, to introduce a child to his first day at school, to speak the right words to a bereaved friend.

Once when this lady, her husband and their small son were traveling along a desert stretch in the Southwestern part of the United States, the brakes on their car suddenly gave way. As the small son started declaring aloud "divine order, divine order, divine order," a service station suddenly seemed to "rise" out of the desert. There they found the help needed and learned that this was the only station within 50 miles!

A young couple on the verge of seeking a divorce tried as a last resort affirming "divine order" for their marriage. It was soon transformed into a happy one.

The phrase "divine order" once brought healing to a child who had been unconscious with a high fever and convulsions. In another instance, a young mother who was expecting her first child, had been informed that giving birth to a child would be difficult and that she should expect complications. As she called on "divine order" to heal the situation, all fear left and the baby was delivered whole and perfect.

THE EFFECT OF ORDER ON FEMALE PROBLEMS

Women with female problems or pre-natal birth problems should constantly call on the mind power of order at the navel, since this is the physical as well as the mental and emotional seat of such problems in the body.

When released through affirmation, divine order radiates its mighty power into your other mind powers located in the 11 vital nerve centers of the body, so that wholeness and balance are activated in the mind, emotions and body again.

Just as it is through the nerve center at the navel that the unborn child receives sustenance from the mother, so it is through this mind power of order located at the navel that the soul of man, when quickened by the mind power of order, receives life sustenance, increased vitality, energy and healing power.

OVERCOME CHALLENGES WITH ORDER

Divine order is not hard and binding; it expresses in freedom and joy. One who does not act in accordance with divine order suffers mentally and physically. He fails to grow spiritually and the reaction of the life forces within him can destroy him as they become dammed up in mind and body with no outlet.

Such dammed up life forces become negative and burn up energy. Negative emotions also prevent the body from renewing and rebuilding itself. To retain animosities of any kind seals up the poisons in the body, and these poisons then generate new poisons.

What is the remedy for all this? Accentuate the positive by decreeing divine order. This eliminates the negative emotions from mind and body and makes way for miraculous changes to take place!

Also, the mind power of order working in the subconsciousness unearths buried talents, reveals hidden powers, and opens the way for their expression. *The mind power of order coordinates all the mind powers so that new inspirations may spring forth and find unhindered recognition in the conscious mind. Order releases the overcoming power of man. You can overcome much in life that challenges you just by affirming "divine order."*

TURNING FAILURE INTO SUCCESS

I once met a fine businessman who was one of the most calm, harmonious, peaceful people I've ever known. He had made a fortune after taking up the study of the power of thought, following a career of total failure. I soon discovered that his constant radiations of peace, poise and power were due to his decrees of "divine order."

No matter what happened in this man's life or in the lives of those about him, he would always decree that everything was in divine order. This attitude gave him a sense of dominion and control over his life that most folks just never acquire. In that state of mind it seemed easy for him to go on to enjoy the health, wealth and happiness that many people seek in a frantic, hectic, misguided way.

Developing the mind power of order abolishes fear and despair, sickness and weakness. Health and freedom are the natural outworking of order. Affirming order releases it to working in the subconscious areas of the body, where it eliminates that which is weak and negative. Then a yoking and pulling together of all your mind powers takes place, so that both soul and body are uplifted and healed. Among the disciples of Jesus was James, son of Alphaeus, symbolizing the mind power of order. His work was to cooperate with the other disciples.

By deliberately developing your mind power of order, you discover it to be a faculty that moves the machinery of mind, body and affairs more perfectly, scientifically, harmoniously, and skillfully than the most effective stage manager handles a play.

HOW TO QUICKEN THIS HEALING
FACULTY OF ORDER

The center of order in the body of man, located at the nerve center back of the navel, is quickened by prayer, meditation and affirmation. Divine order then radiates its mighty power into the other faculties and sets them into sustained activity, so that harmony and wholeness are the natural result in man's mind, body and affairs. Through developing the mind power of order, the greatness of both soul and body is demonstrated. Affirm often that your "house" (state of mind) is in order and all the forces of your being are working to glorify the good in your life.

There is a law of spiritual and mental growth constantly at work in your mind. You are not liberated from all your problems by a sudden, violent overcoming, but by a steady step-by-step unfoldment of order in mind and body.

The forces of Divine Intelligence located in the Christ Mind at the crown of the head are so intense and powerful that the outer consciousness cannot stand the full current all at once. If this dynamic energy were instantly poured forth from the crown of the head into the entire body, its current would be so strong that it would destroy the organism! Through the more gradual, evolutionary adjustment of the natural man, this mighty current not only preserves, but raises up the substance and life of your organism naturally and normally. *This is the work of your healing power of divine order as it unfolds within you gradually but thoroughly for your highest good.*

Man is a powerhouse, generating and giving forth energies at all times. Dwelling on "order" releases these energies in a constructive way. A lady attending a lecture on order decided to test its power immediately. As her companion coughed, she affirmed "divine order" silently, and the coughing ceased.

An overworked mother developed diarrhea. Within 20 minutes from the time she began affirming "DIVINE ORDER NOW PREVAILS IN ALL FUNCTIONS AND ACTIVITIES," the condition was gone. Arising from her bed, she then went forth quietly setting her household in divine order, so there was no further need for the overwork and the anxiety that had made her sick in the first place.

DEMONSTRATE GOOD HEALTH
THROUGH DIVINE ORDER

If you desire to demonstrate health, you must order your life rightly by decreeing divine order, for if its mental and physical activities are not so ordered, discord will ensue. Everything must be brought into order. If you are affirming healing and prosperity, but are still holding on to disorganized thoughts, this will produce inharmony and discord of body and affairs. *Lack of orderly arrangement of one's thoughts is responsible for many delayed demonstrations of healing.*

As you begin developing your mind power of order, you will come into a new state of thought and action, and find yourself doing many things differently because the orderly mind power that directs the universe is now working through you. A harmonious relationship will be established in all your ways. Whatever there was in mind, body or affairs that was out of harmony will easily be adjusted, as you open the way in your mind for the manifestation of divine order.

Just as there is necessity for law and order in prenatal culture in order to give birth to a healthy child, so there is necessity for law and order in the mind of man to re-establish health in his body.

CHANGES YOU CAN EXPECT
FROM DIVINE ORDER

As you affirm divine order for healing in the body, your taste for foods will probably change. You will desire only the purest and best foods that are conducive to good health. People who are trying to lose weight, or to stop smoking or drinking should affirm divine order. They will then find their false appetites disappearing, and their health problems with them. As long as you believe in the slow processes of what is called "nature" you place yourself under a law of slowness. But if you will begin anew and affirm divine order, you will find yourself operating under a different and higher law.

If there is a tendency to hurry, stop and affirm divine order. Rest yourself in its poise. There is no need to hurry. You are living in eternity now and always will be. If you have been disorderly and indefinite, put yourself at once under the decree of divine order, and the same law that keeps the stars operating harmoniously will begin working in and through your life and affairs, making all things right. *You make living cells through the power of your thought. Orderly thoughts make orderly cells. The mind draws upon the vital forces and, according to one's thoughts, alters the tissues of the body.* You constantly tear down or build up your health according to the nature of your thinking.

THE INFINITE BLESSINGS OF DIVINE ORDER

Get your mind in divine order and a mighty mind force will begin to work for you immediately. This divine order is necessary to the building up of both mind and body. Divine order is a vigorous stimulant. It uplifts the whole consciousness, vitalizing the organs, and giving you courage and endurance. It also tends to make you supersensitive to divine healing currents!

As this happens, be on the alert to see harmony everywhere. Do not magnify seeming differences. Do not give your attention to pettiness in people or situations, but continually declare universal harmony. Declare, "I AM IN TRUE RELATIONSHIP WITH ALL PEOPLE AND ALL

SITUATIONS NOW." This will insure perfect, divine order and wholeness of mind and body.

It is thus as you unify your mind powers through divine order, that your body is lifted up into a new state of harmony. Oceans of medications are swallowed daily, millions of doctors are exerting their energies, and prayers unnumbered go forth to wipe out disease. Yet calling on the mind power of "order" is all powerful in fulfilling this universal need of mankind.

As you daily affirm "divine order," you will begin to see the fruitful results made apparent by the mental currents that you set up about you. You may not be able to point out just how each decree brought an effect, but as the months go by you will gradually observe the various changes that are taking place in your mind, body, and affairs. You will find that your outlook on life has broadened immensely. Your little, limited world has been transformed into a bigger, more worthwhile world!

Your mind will become more alert, your body more vital, and you will be free from inharmony and weakness. You will no longer be fearful, frittering your time and energy away on little things. You will become aware that there is a divine hand guiding the universe and you. This will give you a sense of cosmic security. This sense of security will extend to your health and affairs, as you no longer will worry about them. There will be an absence of prejudice and faultfinding in you. You will no longer judge harshly. You will be more generous, and others will respond by being more generous toward you. Things will come your way which previously seemed withheld from you.

Not only will these vast improvements show forth in your particular life and affairs, but you will observe its quiet effect upon those about you. They will become happier, more harmonious, and healthier in mind and body. It is then that you will know the magic power that has been released in those two heavenly words "divine order."

AN AGGRAVATED BLADDER CONDITION HEALED

A nurse named Clara Palmer was healed of an incurable disease through prayer. Thereafter she became a spiritual healer and witnessed the remarkable healings of many supposed incurable diseases. In her book, *You Can Be Healed,*[1] she wrote: "Divine order rules the body."

She then related the case of a patient, suffering from cystitis, who was unhappy, nervous, and irritable. Mrs. Palmer realized that the patient's own lack of orderly thinking had contributed to this bladder condition.

She told the patient she must cast off irritability and unhappy thought habits, as well as casting off unneeded things in her outer world, in order to produce an orderly healing.

The woman shrieked, "Cast off things! Do you know that is all my life has been — a dumping ground for cast-off things? Even though we had abundance when I was a child, my thrifty parents thought I should finish wearing out my sister's outgrown clothing. Even the house I live in is one unwanted by the rest of the family. All I ever had was cast-off crusts!"

It was pointed out that the bladder trouble indicated a need for letting go fluids no longer needed by the body. The harm of holding on to anything no longer needed was explained and that, right away, any surplus must be disposed of.

---

1. Clara Palmer, *You Can Be Healed* (Unity Village, MO.: Unity School of Christianity, 1937).

This previously sick, nervous, irritable woman got interested in disposing of the cast-offs her family had dumped on her. As she began directing her surplus toward those who could use it, her life changed for the better. She began letting go of anxious, disturbing, unkind, unjust thoughts.

Gradually this woman became less irritable, unhappy and nervous as she acquired a deeper understanding and patience. Then came a time when she slept the night through with no irritation or pain. Acidity disappeared from her system, and finally the bladder that had troubled her for years began to function properly. As she brought order into her mind and surroundings, she was happier in mind and more comfortable in body than she had been in years. One of the prayers used had been: "THE INFLOW AND OUTFLOW OF EVERYTHING IN MY LIFE IS ESTABLISHED IN DIVINE ORDER AND HARMONY. I AM PEACEFUL AND POISED."

If you need order in your life, affirm the following, "EVERY ORGAN OF MY BODY IS UNDER DIVINE ORDER. HABITS OF CLEANLINESS, COMFORT AND ORDER ARE NOW ESTABLISHED, AND I AM GOD'S WHOLE AND PERFECT CHILD."

AN OXFORD GRADUATE PROVED
THE JOYS OF DIVINE ORDER

When you affirm order, it has a coordinating effect upon your mind and body. Your mind powers begin to work in harmony within and all around you. There is nothing new about this idea of divine order and of the power it has to work apparent miracles in our lives.

Many years ago the father of American psychology, William James, related how an Oxford graduate heard about the power of divine order and decided to experiment with it.

This Oxford graduate began decreeing divine order for his life, but with fear and trembling, because he had the erroneous idea that God's will meant something positively unpleasant. He assumed that by affirming divine order, the results might not be too satisfying, but being greatly in need of life's blessings, he decided to risk the results.

To his complete surprise, this young man found that as he decreed order, his bad habits left him; his despair dissolved; his character and body were strengthened; and his whole being was infused with a radiance and a power he had never before known. Affirming divine order proved to be a thoroughly enjoyable, satisfying and healing experience.

HOW DIVINE ORDER CAN BRING MUCH GOOD TO YOU

So it can be with you! These are two words, *Divine Order,* that can bring much good to you. Use the phrase as a healing one. As you do so continually, a pattern of perfection can be established. When there is a need for inspiration, continual adjustment, increasing prosperity, spiritual discernment or harmony, in your affairs, dwelling on divine order is the answer. It can also lead to right relations with your family, friends and co-workers.

When the demands become too great and the tension mounts, you will be shown how to free yourself of all that is unnecessary with these words. A family threatened with eviction and lawsuit affirmed divine order, and the lawsuit soon faded away.

I have found that if I tape the words "divine order" to my telephone, only necessary calls come through.

If you have financial challenges, place the words "divine order" near your check book, wallet or unpaid bills. As you pay the bills affirm divine order, and you will be shown exactly how to meet your financial affairs in the best way. It is as though substance stretches for you, or multiples for you, or rearranges itself to meet your needs through divine order.

I have found that when I am feeling pressed or pressured with my work, if I will place the words "divine order" near where I plan to study, write or counsel, somehow things and people quietly conform to that idea.

I recall once having a piece of work to do and thought, "This will probably take a couple of days, and I do not have a couple of days to devote to this project. But it must get done regardless." Then I remembered to write out the words "divine order" in big bold print and place them near my desk.

After beginning the project, I looked at those words often for encouragement. The project got done quickly, easily and completely in only half a day. There were no interruptions and the ideas flowed freely, arranging themselves in perfect sequence. That is the power of divine order!

ONE OF THE HIGHEST FORMS OF PRAYER

One of the highest forms of prayer is to give thanks for divine order in your mind, body and affairs, whether it seems to be there or not. As you begin to call on order located at the nerve center back of the navel, you will find yourself getting into the stream of divine order.

First you will get a sense of peace, power, control of your mind and emotions. Then you will just begin to feel better both emotionally and physically. Situations may still be the same, but they no longer overwhelm you.

Next, you will find yourself feeling compelled to do things in an outer way that will put your affairs in order.

You may feel like cleaning house or setting up a new bookkeeping system in your financial affairs. You may feel led to rearrange your daily schedule or other things in your life. You may get busy in an outer way on previously contemplated tasks. Suddenly you will know what to do and will sail forth in eager anticipation to do it.

One of the finest ways you can help others is by decreeing divine order for them, too. If you are concerned about a loved one, relative, business associate or friend, bless him or her with divine order. If you feel that this person would be happier with more understanding, new strength, a better position, added friends, a fuller life, or more of any good thing, then see him established in divine order.

Bless the world about you unselfishly with divine order. For a drought-stricken area that needs rain, for protection of crops, freedom from pests, or when floods or storms threaten lives and property, *declare divine order.* For political affairs or world peace affirm divine order.

As you do, you release the healing power of order into the atmosphere to do its perfect work, while you personally gain freedom from fear and a new sense of security and protection. Look for, expect, and give thanks for *divine order* often. By doing so, you release one of your most important mind powers to work for you and through you to bless yourself and all mankind.

Your healing power of

ZEAL

— 11 —

Have you ever tried to get someone else to think the way you thought he should, only to get a stiff neck for your trouble? Or have you tried to convince another to do what you wanted him to do, and only got a severe headache at the back of your neck?

If so, you have misused your mind power of *zeal* that is located at the base of the brain, and it was letting you know it!

Zeal is a very special mind power that releases a certain type of energy needed for the mind, body and personality of man.

The ancients felt that zeal was a special gift from God, conferred only upon a select few. The reason they felt zeal to be so special was because the ancient seers noticed that zealous persons seemed stirred by a "certain something," which made them different from ordinary men and that gave them a strange power of accomplishment. They considered it a fire from heaven, calling it the "divine afflatus," which they believed would consume that which was worthless and purify the soul, leaving it cleansed of stupidity and ready to express great ideas and talents, making those so endowed mental and spiritual giants.

The ancient seers were partially right: People who have developed the mind power known as zeal *do* seem to have a special energy and power that makes them different from the masses; they *do* seem to have strange powers of accomplishment as the "divine afflatus" cleanses their minds and emotions, leaving them free to express ideas and talents that may even lead to greatness; and they *do* differ from the masses who are inclined to be listless, inactive and prone to wait for some outer power or event to stir them into action.

But the marvelous truth is that we all have this "certain something"—this "divine afflatus"—this special energy and talent that can incite us to glorious achievement. We only need to know how to recognize, release and direct it!

CAUSE OF HEALTH PROBLEMS IN THE NECK

It is significant that the mind power of zeal is located at the back of the neck, because the neck is a symbol of the gracious, flexible state of mind. (See Figure 11-1.) Solomon advised: "Keep sound wisdom and discretion; so shall they be life unto thy soul and grace to thy neck." (Proverbs 3:21,22) A gracious, flexible attitude working in a person's interior nature manifests as compassion and love, which is symbolized in a graceful neck.

Graciousness forgives without a thought of there being anything to forgive. To be gracious is to be yielding,

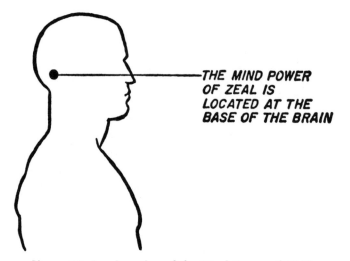

THE MIND POWER OF ZEAL IS LOCATED AT THE BASE OF THE BRAIN

Figure 11–1.   Location of the Mind Power of ZEAL.

nonresistant. The neck is a marvelous combination of yielding nonresistance, since it is able to turn in every direction. In good health it is strong, flexible and bends easily.

When one has health problems in the area of the neck, he is misusing his mind power of zeal. He is fighting, resisting, rebelling against someone or some circumstance of life, and has probably become intolerant. His stiffened attitudes literally manifest as a stiff neck!

There once was a woman who constantly had serious family problems. For 15 years she had suffered a stiff neck in spite of the finest treatment. Finally the metaphysical source of this woman's health problems became apparent. *She was totally intolerant of new ideas.*

Every time the prospering, healing law of *tithing* was mentioned in church, this woman took it as a personal offense and did not return for months. Though she had grave health and family problems, she refused to even consider the great law of tithing as a possible solution.

Secretly, of course, she knew she should be putting God first in every phase of her life, and since she was not, it was her own secret guilt that offended her most. This reaction was an indication of her unusual "stiffening" in mind and body to new ideas.

This lady might well have lived in the days of Jeremiah, who advised his followers: "Hallow ye the sabbath day, as I commanded your father. But they hearkened not, neither inclined their ear, but made their neck stiff, that they might not hear, and might not receive instructions." (Jeremiah 17:22, 23)

The disciple symbolizing zeal was Simon the Canaanite later called "Simon the Zealot." "Simon" means "hearing." How often we are like the stiff-necked woman, and in our zealousness refuse to "hear" the Truth.

PSYCHOLOGICAL MAKEUP OF STIFF-NECKED PEOPLE

The Bible describes the psychological makeup of stiff-necked people. Moses admonished the Israelites: "I know thy rebellion, and thy stiff neck." (Deuteronomy 31:27) Nevertheless, he prayed for those headstrong, disobedient people asking Jehovah to forgive their inflexibility: "If now I have found favor in thy sight, O Lord, I pray thee, go in the midst of us; for it is a stiff-necked people; and pardon our iniquity and our sin, and take us for thine inheritance." (Exodus 34:9) Jehovah advised, "Circumcise therefore the foreskin of your heart and be not more stiff-necked." (Deuteronomy 10:16) The act of circumcision is the act of cutting off, and it symbolizes cutting off arrogant, disobedient, intolerant, critical states of mind.

The Psalmist abased the arrogant and over-zealous: "I said unto the arrogant, Deal not arrogantly. And to the wicked. . . Speak not with a stiff neck." (Psalms 75:4,5)

Hezekiah warned the Hebrews of his time, "Now be ye not stiff-necked, as your fathers; but yield yourselves unto Jehovah." (II Chronicles 30:8)

The zealous Stephen lamented just before his stoning, "Ye stiff-necked . . . in heart and ears, ye do always resist the Holy Spirit, as your fathers did." (Acts 7:51)

Always the psychological makeup of these people was the same. They wanted their own way in every situation, usually zealously trying to force it. They were intolerant of new ideas; they refused to consider another's viewpoint.

A zealous woman learned of the power of thought and immediately tried to change her husband's thinking, instead of working to improve her own. The result? She constantly suffered from a stiff neck!

HEALING FOR THE STIFF-NECKED

When the neck needs healing, let the sufferer ask himself, "Am I gracious to all? Am I nonresistant, flexible, uncondemning? Do I try to force others to think and do as I say? Am I resisting the guidance of that still, small voice of Truth within me?" *The stiff-necked Israelites stopped their good and were long delayed in their entrance into the Promised Land because of their critical, rebellious attitudes. Many people nowadays never make it into their Promised Land of increased health, wealth and happiness for the same reason.* Like the Hebrews of old they seem to have a "yoke of iron upon their neck." (Deuteronomy 28:48)

Loosen up your human will, and let a flexible, teachable attitude take away every mental quirk and trace of crankiness. Be at peace with God and man, thus maintaining your inner balance. *The neck is the balancing place between the head and heart. The perfect union of intellectual reasoning and intuitive feeling takes place at the neck. It is here that the conscious and subconscious phases of the mind meet.* When man is using his zeal with wisdom, he knows what Job of old meant when he wrote, "In his neck abideth strength." (Job 41:22)

For attaining this peaceful strength, fix your attention at the back of the neck and decree, "I UNLEASH MY SPIRITUAL FORCES. I AM UNFETTERED AND UNBOUND. MY LIFE CANNOT BE LIMITED. MY GOOD CANNOT BE LIMITED. NO FALSE CONDITION HAS ANY POWER OVER ME. I AM FREE WITH THE FREEDOM OF SPIRIT."

TEMPER YOUR ZEAL WITH WISDOM

To be without zeal is to be without a zest for living. Zeal is the impulse to go forward. The word "zeal" means "active interest" and the word "enthusiasm" is one of the highest forms of zeal meaning "to be inspired."

A person without zeal is like an engine without power. But one's zeal must be tempered with wisdom. The mind power of zeal can become so active intellectually that it drains one's vitality and leaves nothing for physical well-being.

Man is a dynamo of pent-up power, but he needs judgment in its use. Be careful not to let your zeal run away with you, getting the best of your judgment. One may become so zealous as to bring on nervous prostration. After such an experience the Psalmist complained, "The zeal of thy house hath eaten me up." (Psalms 69:9)

Anytime the zeal center located at the base of the brain is misused, it reacts. It lets you know you should be tempering your zeal with wisdom.

Zeal's center of activity in the body is at the base of the brain in the medulla oblongata. The vaulted chambers, passageways and mysteries of the brain excited the admiration of the ancients, who felt it had occult significance. The office of the brain located in this area at the back of the neck is to vaporize the fine nerve fluid and distribute it to the senses. The medulla performs in the body a work comparable to that of the carburetor in your automobile, distributing vaporized gasoline.

HEALTH PROBLEMS CAUSED BY OVER-ZEALOUSNESS

In the human body, zeal electrifies the nerve substance, which breaks forth into energy. Thoughts build nerve and brain centers that serve as distributors of the vital substance manufactured by the body. The vitamins in the food that we eat are stored up by the body chemistry and liberated in thought and action by man's zeal. Every thought and emanation of mind liberates some of this stored-up substance.

The mind power of zeal at the base of the brain imparts special energy to the ears, eyes, nose, mouth, and sensory nervous system. (See Figure 11-2.) When you misuse your zeal, either by trying to force your will and your way on someone else, or by burning up this wonderful energy in unwise activities, you get a physical reaction, often through those five senses.

When you burn up your zeal, your eyes may give you trouble, as they get weak or out of focus. You may wonder what is wrong. Nothing serious, usually. You have

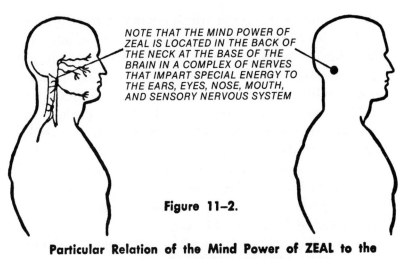

NOTE THAT THE MIND POWER OF ZEAL IS LOCATED IN THE BACK OF THE NECK AT THE BASE OF THE BRAIN IN A COMPLEX OF NERVES THAT IMPART SPECIAL ENERGY TO THE EARS, EYES, NOSE, MOUTH, AND SENSORY NERVOUS SYSTEM

Figure 11–2.

Particular Relation of the Mind Power of ZEAL to the Complex of Nerve Energy.

simply drained your eyes of precious energy they needed to function properly. But by misusing this zeal often enough, your eyes may be badly damaged.

People who become "hard of hearing" are sometimes people who have gotten so zealous in trying to make someone else "hear" their ideas that they become totally incapable of hearing another's ideas; they also become "hard of hearing" the whisperings of intuitive understanding within themselves. Such people need to redirect their zeal within, toward themselves. They need to develop their own mind powers more and release other people to find their own way.

People who have sinus trouble and other types of nose trouble are sometimes people who are zealously sticking their nose in someone else's business, as they work hard to make other people conform to their ideas.

A businessman had had sinus trouble for years. This well-meaning, conscientious man freely gave out advice to everyone. A relative or friend could not go near him without his planning out that person's entire life, informing him just what he should do next. His dominating possessiveness was doubtless connected with the persistent trouble he suffered with his eyes and sinuses.

Misusing one's zeal often affects the throat. If you have ever gotten a sore throat for no apparent reason, check to see if you did not try to convince someone else to do what you wanted him to do; perhaps, you spoke negatively with strong feeling and conviction to him. Also, you may have depleted your energy in unwise activity and suffered throat trouble as a result.

There once was a woman who constantly cleared her throat. She took various medications and treatments for throat irritation. A person of dominating personality, she often irritated other people as she tried zealously to control them. The result was that, in turn, she invariably suffered irritation in the throat near the zeal center.

Zealous people often have trouble with their teeth. Of course, an incessant flow of negative words affect the teeth, which need a lot of energy in order to function properly. They are constantly being used, not only through eating, but throughout the day as one speaks forth many words. When the teeth do not receive a normal amount of nerve energy, which comes to them from the zeal centers, they become starved. Cavities, soft teeth and soft gums are the result.

When a person has been too zealous in outer activity or through mentally trying to force others to his way, you can always detect it because his voice is weak, often high pitched, denoting lack of emotional control. A person that has been too zealous usually has a "hollow eyed" look about him that indicates weakness. Such a person has lost contact with the inner source of energy and power.

HOW ZEAL AFFECTS YOUR FIVE SENSES

The law of divine enthusiasm, spiritual and mental zeal, is one of the most powerful laws operative in the realm of mind and body. The world has long been zealous in advocating reforms. The trouble with those reforms was that they aimed to change man's ways without first changing his mind and heart.

Since the zeal center in the back of the neck at the base of the brain feeds nerve energy to your five senses, anytime you misuse that nerve energy—drain it or burn it up—then you exhaust nerve energy and it never gets to your ears, eyes, nose, throat or mouth. Your five senses are literally starved and they react upon you with physical ailments.

When your zeal center becomes drained of its own energy and power, it has to take energy from your eyes, ears, nose, throat and mouth, again robbing them.

THE REMEDY FOR DEPLETION OF YOUR ZEAL

Is there a remedy? There certainly is!

When you have trouble in the areas affected by lack of zeal, get quiet and check on yourself to see if you have been zealously involved in unnecessary activities or in trying to force your will on someone else. Since zeal is located in the area of the *conscious* mind, you can *consciously* stir it up!

Center your attention for a moment at the base of the brain and quietly decree that infinite energy and intelligence are pouring forth as zeal into the five senses. Then follow in your imagination or mind's eye, a set of nerves that lead out from the base of the brain to the eyes, ears, nose, tongue and throat area.

As you mentally carry the zeal current from its center at the base of the brain and mentally connect it with the five senses, especially connecting it with the throat area by speaking forth the word "zeal," a mighty vibration is set up that affects your whole nervous system. In this way you can strengthen your voice, revitalize your teeth, and indirectly impart energy to your whole nervous system. Zeal is a great and all-powerful stimulator.

You cannot think of or repeat the word "zeal" without evoking a certain mental thrill that spurs you into action as you decree it over and over. Every word you speak goes forth from your mouth charged with atomic energies that affect your whole organism.

As you develop your various mind powers, the zeal center comes alive more and more. You can actually feel the mighty power and current of zeal as it works at the back of the neck. It often becomes active as you think, read, study, meditate and make your affirmations. You can then direct that zealous energy mentally to your five senses and to your whole body.

The person who says, "I don't have any energy," is the person who has either misdirected his zeal or has just never developed it. Listless people should affirm often: "I STIR UP THE ZEAL WITHIN ME, AND I AM BLESSED ON EVERY HAND WITH HAPPINESS, SUCCESS AND TRUE ACHIEVEMENT."

A SPECIAL POWER FOR GETTING WHAT YOU WANT

Inner zeal is the power that transforms one! Zeal is the power that incites the other mind powers to greater and greater development. Zeal gives luster, color, and radiance to the personality just as the sparkle of a diamond gives it beauty.

Zeal gives you a certain attractive, magnetic quality that causes your good to rush to you from many directions. A person who is developing his zeal, tempering it with a quiet wisdom, is pretty special. He has a certain vitality that the average person lacks. This extraordinary vibration gives him that indescribable "certain something" for which all people long.

This happens because in the human body, zeal electrifies the nerve substance, which breaks forth into energy. It is then that man radiates an electrical magnetism instantly felt by those about him.

But the person who has not tempered his zeal with wisdom has a certain lack of vitality that is a repelling power. A secretary quit her job when her superiors changed. Her former boss had been a zealous, magnetic person who radiated an enthusiasm and excitement for life that made even daily routine work interesting. The man replacing him seemed almost stupid in his listless reaction to everything. This secretary explained, "There just wasn't any fire in that job anymore. It had no spark, no interest, no appeal."

A famous insurance executive, who went from rags to riches in just ten years, said that his success secret had been his zeal expressing itself as enthusiasm. He stated that enthusiasm is the key to success in life; that without the inner fire stirred up by enthusiasm, a person does not succeed in life no matter how hard he tries. The reason that the person without zeal doesn't succeed in life no matter how sincere he may be is that he is missing that magnetic quality that attracts and excites people into creative action.

Charles Fillmore, known for his zeal, was still affirming it at the age of 94. "I FAIRLY SIZZLE WITH ZEAL AND ENTHUSIASM, AND I SPRING FORTH WITH A MIGHTY FAITH TO DO THE THINGS THAT OUGHT TO BE DONE BY ME."

One of Paul's magnetic qualities as a great apostle was his zeal. He used the word "zeal" frequently in his writings. It was Paul's zeal that carried the Gospel to the entire ancient world. The Bible says that Paul had zeal for God. Had it not been for this great man's zealous intensity, Christianity might never have gotten out of the Holy Land and could have faded away within a few decades. However, Paul learned the necessity for balancing one's zeal with wisdom, because he complained to the Corinthians, "Your zeal provoked many." (II Corinthians 9:2)

ZEAL IS A QUIET, STAYING POWER THAT PRODUCES RESULTS

One of the magnetic qualities of the zealous is that they are quiet people who do not dissipate their zeal with needless activity or talk. We have often mistakenly regarded zeal and enthusiasm as a loud, boisterous quality.

Not so! Zeal is a silent, steady, persistent mind power that gives you dominion and control of your world. True zeal expressing through quietness overcomes seemingly insurmountable obstacles with its mighty energy of purpose. The reason zeal has such power is because it continues on and on quietly, without intermission, until it completes a task.

Instead of starting off with a bang and then promptly running down without finishing a task, zeal has staying power. It has the unique ability to hold on and keep on going until the goal is reached and one has crossed the finish line to results. Zeal produces completion. Anytime you do not seem able to complete a task, that is the time to affirm zeal, declaring: "THIS IS THE TIME OF DIVINE COMPLETION. THE 'ZEAL OF HOSTS' IS COMPLETING THIS NOW."[1]

Zeal not only works in you as energy, right attitudes, action, and staying power, but zeal also works sometimes as a quiet kind of pressure. When you feel an inner pressure working on you, causing you to become dissatisfied with your life and desiring to expand it, your zeal faculty is coming alive, progressively trying to lead you into a better life.

When you feel as though a special kind of energy is pressing upon you, that pressure is often felt in the area of the lungs and you cannot breathe easily. You may feel that quiet pressure upon you to improve your life, possibly to make what seem to be great changes, and your zeal will not let up on its inner pressure until you follow through on its guidance. Such pressure is new good pressing upon you, seeking birth in your life.

Since zeal is not a loud, boisterous, disorganized quality, but a quiet, steady and persistent power, it gives one dominion and control. Zeal works on you and through you continually as you activate it. Once awakened, it will not let up or give up until it has had its way in your life, even though its way makes great demands upon you.

When I have felt the pressure of quiet zeal working within me, I have followed its promptings, though it often meant great changes in my thinking and way of life. Always my zeal knew best and quietly led me into paths of greater good.

---

1. See the chapter on Completion in *The Millionaire Moses*.

You can trust your zeal! You can trust its pressure upon and within you. Zeal is one of your most special mind powers, as it gives you a certain vitality, keenness of mind, magnetism, and a special ability to achieve your heart's desires that none of your other mind powers can!

We all want a zeal for the good in life. For that purpose, center your attention at the base of your brain near the back of the neck and affirm: "I STIR UP THE GIFTS OF GOD WITHIN ME. I AM FILLED WITH ZEAL AND ENTHUSIASM. I SPRING FORTH WITH A MIGHTY FAITH TO DO THE THINGS THAT OUGHT TO BE DONE BY ME."

Unfolding one's mind powers comes in degrees of normality, so do not try to force your zeal to develop. To do so would result in a wrenched nervous system and a depletion in all the five senses. Instead, affirm the activity of zeal in your life. Then *let* it come alive within you as it sees fit.

PRAISE—THE GREAT STIMULATOR OF ZEAL

Never repress the impulse and force of zeal as it wells up within you. Commune with it and praise it for its great energy and efficiency as it works in your mind and body.

Words of praise release the pent-up zeal in man. Words of praise stir up zeal and connect it with the infinite intelligence in the spiritual center at the crown of the head. *Energy is zeal set in motion and words of praise stir up this energy.*

Words of praise also cause a bursting forth of joy in man. Any time you feel depressed declare, "I PRAISE MY MIND AS THE PERFECT CREATION OF DIVINE SUBSTANCE

NOW. I PRAISE MY EMOTIONS AS THE PERFECT CREATION OF DIVINE SUBSTANCE NOW. I PRAISE MY BODY AS THE PERFECT CREATION OF DIVINE SUBSTANCE NOW. I PRAISE MY HEALTH AS THE PERFECT CREATION OF DIVINE SUBSTANCE NOW. I PRAISE MY WORLD AS THE PERFECT CREATION OF DIVINE SUBSTANCE NOW. I NOW SEE MORE GOOD IN MY LIFE THAN I HAVE EVER SEEN BEFORE!"

It will be as though a "holy joy" wells up within you, giving you new hope, new energy, new happiness. Praise also kindles enthusiasm and engenders life as it sets energy free in mind and body. *Praise is the great releaser of energy in mind and body.*

In the time of Moses, he pointed out to the Israelites what happened to those who did not develop a joyous, praiseful state of mind, and even how the zeal center in the neck was literally affected:

"Because thou servest not Jehovah thy God with a joyfulness, and with gladness of heart, by the reason of the abundance of all things. . . he shall put a yoke of iron upon thy neck. Therefore shalt thou serve thine enemies in hunger, and in thirst, and in nakedness, and in want of all things." (Deuteronomy 28:47,48)

Many diseases come from the lack of the expression of joy.[2] *The object of praise is to "let out" an inner joy too long pent up in man.*

The effect of praise on man's body is a response in every cell. Praise redeems one from weariness. In an atmosphere of praise, each cell builds new strength and energy. Since each cell is intelligent and has unlimited power, when praised as perfect, it responds by getting rid of all that is foreign and imperfect and then builds divine perfection in the mind and body of man.

---

2. See the chapter on Joy in *The Prosperity Secrets of the Ages.*

Since praise increases life and energy, it makes for perfect bodily functioning too. Indeed, praise is the connecting link between the powerhouse of God and the body of man.

As praise calls forth the life force in man, it affects three of his mind powers prominently: the zeal center at the back of the head; the power center in the throat; the life center in the generative organs of the abdominal region. An acceleration of zeal often brings healings in any of these areas; it is sure to step up the energy for health there.[3]

Praise is contagious and lifts man's consciousness to lofty levels. On such a level, disease, inharmony and lack fade away. By watching, expecting, and praising every little sign of improved health, man releases his mind power of zeal to heal him. Through practice, man can educate himself to sing, laugh, praise and expect the blessings of life to come his way.

As you pour forth praise with feeling, like Isaiah of old, you will find yourself "clad with zeal as a mantle." (Isaiah 59:17)

---

3. See the chapter on Praise in *The Dynamic Laws of Healing.*

Your healing power of

ELIMINATION

— 12 —

There once was a young churchman who decided to "jazz up religion" in his church. He "went modern" by taking out the church pews and installing bucket seats, by replacing the choir with folk music, and finally, by installing a drive-in window for a confessional.

His congregation, which was used to his antics, didn't bat an eye at all the changes, and everything went along fine until his superior came to visit.

After viewing all the radical changes that were made, the superior said, "I don't mind your taking out the church pews and installing bucket seats. Neither do I object to your replacing that terrible choir with "way out" music. And the drive-in window for confessional may not be a bad idea, either. But there's one thing I do strongly object to: That sign over the drive-in confessional has to go!"

Astounded, the young churchman protested, "What's wrong with the sign over the drive-in confessional?"

The superior stormed, "Just look at it! It says 'Toot and tell—or go to hell!'"

However, in these times there are a lot of people who need to "toot and tell." The healing law of elimination helps you do just that.

WHERE THE MIND POWER OF ELIMINATION IS LOCATED

The mind power of elimination is located as shown in Figure 12-1 in the organs of elimination. In the lower part of the back, near the base of the spinal column, is the nerve center which presides over the elimination of waste from the body. This nerve center also presides over the elimination of waste from man's thoughts and emotions.

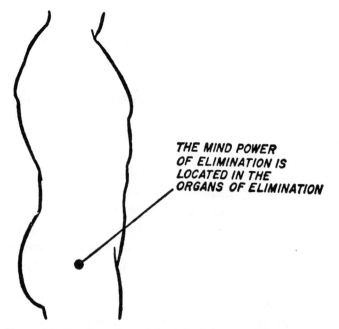

THE MIND POWER OF ELIMINATION IS LOCATED IN THE ORGANS OF ELIMINATION

Figure 12–1. Location of the Mind Power of ELIMINATION.

People who suffer from physical ailments in the organs of elimination in the abdominal region of the body are people who need to release and eliminate some negative emotions. Perhaps, they need to eliminate some possessive attitudes or relationships from their lives.

People who hold on tightly and possessively to that which is no longer for their highest good suffer the most from physical ailments in the organs of elimination. Also, people who are tightly possessed by others can suffer accordingly, even when it is done in the name of "love." Kidney trouble, disease in the colon and intestinal tract, liver ailments, diabetic conditions, hemorrhoids, constipation, are all caused by holding to thoughts, feelings, experiences, or people that need to be emotionally released.

Possessiveness, which is one of the worst forms of bondage causing all kinds of health, financial and human relations problems, is often reflected in the organs of elimination as disease.[1]

HEALING FROM POSSESSIVENESS

A lady once visited a spiritual counselor, stating that her brother was very ill in the hospital. Because of his age, his doctors would not operate and gave no hope of his recovery from an intestinal disease.

The counselor learned something of the interior nature of this man: He was a very lovable relative, yet much attached to money, possessions and to the people he loved, especially to one sister who nursed him. He constantly demanded her attention.

---

1. See the chapter, "Love Works a Healing Power," in *The Prospering Power of Love.*

The one seeking help for him was advised to declare that her brother was free from every attachment: "THE CHRIST LOVE IN YOU, IMPERSONAL AND UNMIXED, DISSOLVES ALL APPEARANCES OF SELFISHNESS IN YOU NOW, AND THE PURE, SELFLESS LOVE OF CHRIST TAKES ITS PLACE. YOU ARE NOW FREE IN MIND AND BODY."

In a few days the man was feeling much improved and in a short time he was walking quite comfortably. In a few months a perfect healing had taken place in his body and even his disposition had changed as he had become less demanding.

Later, in reflecting upon his healing, this man said that one day while in meditation, the Christ spirit had seemed close to him. Then there had been a feeling of loosening up, both mentally and physically. At that moment he knew the healing of the intestines had taken place.

As this man proved, *the first organs in the body that are affected by the lifting up of the mind are the organs of elimination!*

Affirm often, "I NOW WILLINGLY LET GO EVERY THOUGHT, CONDITION, OR RELATIONSHIP THAT IN ANY WAY RETARDS MY PERFECT HEALING. I AM BLESSED WITH PERFECT ELIMINATION IN MIND, BODY, AFFAIRS AND RELATIONSHIPS NOW!"

EFFECTS OF WILLPOWER ON ELIMINATION

Since the mind power of elimination and renunciation is located in the lower abdominal region of the body, it is located in the seat of the subconscious mind. Not only does the job of elimination include renouncing, dissolving and eliminating all waste products from the body, but also all negative emotions stored in the subconscious, *emotional* region in the abdomen.

The intellectual center in man is located in the head; the affectional center in man is located at the heart; the sensual center in man is located in the abdomen. A famous author who had written many sensual books recently passed on from liver trouble located in the sensual area of the body.

This nerve center is very sensitive to thoughts about substance, money, finances and the material world. *A gripping mental hold on material things will cause constriction in this abdominal area. It takes relaxation in mind, and a loosening of one's grip on material possessions to bring freedom from constriction and renewed health in the abdominal area of the body.*

One reason for many of these ills is that the mind power of elimination located in the nerve center in the lower part of the back near the base of the spine is closely connected with the mind-power of will located in the top of the front forehead. The will, operating through the front brain, controls circulation of life in the whole body.

A tense will that is determined to have its own way, constricts and congests all the functions of the body. A set determination can so constrict the faculty of elimination that it cannot cast off waste products from the body. In fact, a tense personality will cause a slowing down process in the whole body, so that there is a lessening of energy and vitality.

A willful holding on to material things will cause constriction in the organs of elimination because *it is the duty of the elimination to release and let go, rather than to hold on to substance.*

The set determination to succeed in some chosen field of action, study, profession, business or personal ambition calls most of the body energy to the head, and starves the mind powers located in the chest and abdominal regions. School children are crammed with worldly knowledge and are spurred on to make high grades. This forces the blood to the head and depletes its flow into the abdominal region.

Sometimes you find that when you do concentrated mental work, the blood is forced into the area of the conscious mind in your front forehead and causes headaches. Then, that lack of blood in the abdominal area causes tension, friction and discomfort there.

The overflow of life, blood and energy to the will center in the front forehead can cause enlarged adenoids, inflamed tonsils, sinus trouble, and other ills of the head, while the abdominal region suffers from constipation and general lack of vital action.

RELAXATION OF THE WILL HEALS

The remedy for these conditions is relaxation of the will, and the "letting go" of purely personal objectives. Relaxation of the tense abdomen depends upon relaxation of a tense will. The practice of relaxing and mentally distributing your nerve energy throughout the body should become a habit in daily meditation periods. Deliberately start at the top of the head and go slowly down through the body, decreeing: "RELAX AND LET GO." Drop from mind the attitude of having so much to do, of being crowded and pushed with work. Say quietly, "NOT BY POWER NOR BY MIGHT, BUT BY GOD'S SPIRIT WITHIN, THIS IS BEING DONE."

Your willful affirmation can produce a congested condition throughout the body and interfere with elimination, if it is used in a strenuous, tense, and willful way. It is wise to use affirmations in a relaxed way and after having used them continuously for a time, then release them to do their perfect work in the subconscious.

Continued strenuous and strained affirmations tend to cause constriction in the elimination mind center. The remedy is to relax, to let go. Your words of healing must have enough time to work out in the subconscious phases of your being.

It is possible to overload the mind just as it is possible to overload the stomach. Thoughts must be digested in a manner similar to the way in which food is digested. Without their proper digestion and assimilation, your thoughts can end in mental congestion, confusion, and frustration.

THE MENTAL CAUSES OF MANY BROKEN HIPS

Sometimes one's will has been resisted so persistently by another's will that curvature of the spine may develop. Perverse wills, full of domination, leave their mark on their owners in the lower back and spine. Also, a sense of excessive burden bearing, typical of the depressed, cynical state of mind, causes the back to almost bend double as one carries his problems in a mental sack on his back.

Little ol' ladies who break their hips are often people who have dominated their families. As they grow older, no longer having the power to wield over others which they once had, this "breaks them up" emotionally and also physically. Broken hips or other troubles in the lower back and spine are often the result, usually through an "accident."

A very dominating woman lost her power to dictate to another when her husband suddenly passed on. She had always suffered from constipation, hemorrhoids and other "willful" diseases of the abdominal region. She was surprised to realize that she was still as jealous of her husband as when he had been alive and that the cause of her jealousy lay within her own emotions, not within her husband's actions. One day while still in such a brooding, jealous mood over her late husband, she fell and broke a hip.

The hips indicate willfulness and possessiveness and are directly connected with the mind power of will in the front forehead through the spine. Another lady's great wealth was passed on to a relative to control. No longer able to dominate her relatives, friends and employees through her wealth, she felt helpless and "broken up." A broken hip soon followed.

Still another was suffering with a compound curvature of the spine and two vertebrae were standing up and out of line with the rest. On the opposite side a little higher up, there were two more out of position. The flesh around these vertebrae was hot, red, swollen and painful. The sufferer had had osteopathic treatments until the back was inflamed and sore. The last doctor had been unable to get two of these bones into place because the patient's back was too sore to be even slightly touched.

She sought out a spiritual counselor, who affirmed for her:

"THE MEMORIES OF THE PAST HAVE VANISHED AS THE MIST BEFORE THE SUN. GOD IS LOVING YOU, DEAR ONE, INTO YOUR PERFECTION OF BODY WHICH IS NOW GUARDED AND PROTECTED BY THE GOD POWER WITHIN YOU. YOU ARE NOT WEAK-WILLED NOR OBSTINATE IN YOUR HUMAN WILL. GOD'S WILL GOVERNS YOUR MIND SO THAT YOU THINK THE

THOUGHTS OF LOVE, TRUTH AND PURITY. YOU ARE STRAIGHT
AND UPRIGHT IN YOUR CHARACTER. YOU LOVE ALWAYS TO
DO THE RIGHT THING BY EVERYONE WITH WHOM YOU HAVE
ANY DEALINGS, EITHER IN BUSINESS, SOCIALLY OR IN YOUR
HOME LIFE. THERE IS NOTHING UNTRUE ABOUT YOU. NO
CROOKEDNESS EXISTS IN YOUR MIND, BODY OR AFFAIRS. YOU
ARE WHOLE, YOU ARE STRAIGHT, YOU ARE AT PEACE, YOU
ARE FREE."

As the counselor spoke these revealing words, the one
suffering realized some of the obstinate attitudes that
had bound up her back into this painful condition. With
that realization, a great feeling of happiness welled up
within her. Then a "queer" but comfortable feeling flowed
up and down her spine.

Within twenty-four hours, the pain and soreness were
gone. The second and third days brought no change in
the placement of the bones, which were still out of place.
But on the fourth day, she felt a gentle, powerful
feeling—like a soft hand—putting in place each bone
separately, a few seconds apart, and then a tingling sensation like new life passed from one end of her spine to
the other, followed by a warm glow all over, and a sense
of freedom. She had been healed just as simply as that!

CAUSE OF ABDOMINAL DISEASES

*There is no stagnation in a healthy body. Its perfect
system of assimilation and elimination is unequalled by
any invention of man. The body acts with fearlessness
and intelligence in receiving sustenance, and in letting
go of that no longer needed.*

In the wear and tear of living there is a continual accumulation of wastes that must be thrown off, or the
body becomes poisoned and dies. Though there are a

number of excretory organs through which the elimination of useless substance passes, the most important of
these organs are the liver, the kidneys, the lungs, the
perspiratory glands of the skin, and the intestinal tract.

Substances taken into the body that have served their
purposes become devitalized and are no longer connected with the life force in man. The body has to get
rid of these waste products in order to make room for
new life-formed substances.

NEGATIVE EMOTIONS BLOCK NORMAL ELIMINATION

Strongly negative emotions impede the elimination of
used substances from the body and all manner of health
problems then result.

High on the list are strong-willed people who have a
sluggish liver, which is not open and free in action. Any
distress of the mind slows down the liver. Living in the
past, condemning one's self, and regret of the past affects the liver and can even lead to death. Those who
want to take on new ideas, but cannot emotionally turn
loose of old ones have liver trouble. Resentment and pettiness are reflected in the liver, since a healthy liver casts
out the untrue and holds fast to the good. When the liver
is forced to hold to the past regretfully, the kidneys
record this state of mind and become infected by it.

ELIMINATION BY THE SKIN

Need for elimination is reflected in the skin, too, when
the perspiration becomes unwholesome as a result of
gloominess held in mind. One of the functions of the

lungs is to throw off waste vapors. Insufficient breathing in of fresh air causes an overworking of the kidneys, as shown by the density of the urine.

A lady was once healed of a painful skin disease so severe that it had spread over her entire body, even into her hair. Also, a painful kidney condition from which she had suffered for years was healed, as she deliberately fasted for just one month from irritated, critical, disturbed reactions over trivial things.

CAUSES OF SLUGGISH BOWEL INFECTIONS

The bowels also become either constipated or loose due to mental poisons held in mind. A worried mind will inflame the intestines. Some cases of bowel trouble can be traced to a selfish holding to that which should be given to others or in some way passed out of one's life. A miserly man was once healed of a chronic state of constipation by beginning to deliberately give to others, where before he had been mean and niggardly. When you affirm, "DIVINE INTELLIGENCE IS NOW IN CHARGE OF ALL THE FUNCTIONS OF MY BODY," you are shown just what mental or outer action to take to bring about healing.

Hemorrhoids are caused by a clogging of the mind. Irritability, fretfulness, resistance, and anxiety cause constipation which can become chronic. Also, improperly placing one's affections causes hemorrhoids. A widow who had always dominated her husband, suffered constantly from hemorrhoids after his death. Her affections had been improperly placed as she had possessed her husband's spirit, soul and body. Being unable to do so any longer, she was irritable, fretful, anxious, resistant to her new set of circumstances.

RELEASE TENSIONS IN
ORGANS OF ELIMINATION

As this lady proved, tension causes health problems in the organs of elimination. Also, neglecting the inner urge to let go of the old and make room for the new tends to clog one's life with the debris of past mistakes, disappointments, and sufferings. No function of the body teaches this lesson more clearly than the bowels.

Declare often: "I WILLINGLY RELEASE THE THOUGHTS AND THINGS THAT CLUTTER MY LIFE. I FORGIVE MYSELF AND OTHERS, AND I AM FREE FROM ALL MISJUDGMENT, BIT-TERNESS, INJUSTICE, INTOLERANCE, AND REVENGE. EVERY ORGAN OF MY BODY IS QUICKLY BENEFITTED. ALL MISUN-DERSTANDING AND BITTERNESS IS NOW ELIMINATED FROM MY MIND, BODY AND WORLD."

Undue tension and intensity is the cause of many diseased conditions in the abdominal region: fear, over-conscientiousness, anxiety, resentment, and similar con-stricting emotions. *Releasing the past is one of the greatest health aids to all the organs of elimination.* Never try to bring back or to relive old experiences. When tempted to do so affirm, "I PURGE THE MIND OF DEAD THOUGHTS AND DEAD RELATIONSHIPS."

Alkaline conditions in the body seem governed by one's affections, while acid conditions seem governed by one's reasoning nature.

Religious beliefs have a very vital, or devitalizing ef-fect upon the mind and body, especially upon the kidneys which reflect the mind's judgments. The Greek word for "judgment" means "to separate or set apart," and this is the function of the kidneys. If the kidneys get inflamed from severe criticisms, then the liver becomes sympathetically disturbed. *False judgments and criti-cisms are always reflected in the organs of elimination.*

If there seems to be an overworking of the kidneys, then attitudes of criticism, unkindness, sarcasm, cutting remarks, fault-finding, looking for the worst, picking out weaknesses in people, and dwelling on people's short-comings are probably involved. There must be a softening and sweetening of these acid thoughts, as well as a withdrawal of condemnation from one's fellow beings.

A woman who had suffered for years from back and kidney trouble was perfectly healed in just two weeks after she bridled her tongue and refrained from cutting criticism, sarcasm, and condemnation. With practice and patience she eventually developed a sweet disposition that added immeasurably to a wholesome life.

A floating kidney can be traced to a mixed, uncertain, weak judgment which never makes anything clear. A housewife once suffered from this condition after her husband got interested in another woman. He seemed to have a mixed, uncertain feeling about the affair and never made anything clear about whether he would leave or stay with his wife. His mixed uncertainty reflected in his wife's health.

When one becomes uplifted, dwells upon the good in himself and others, and refrains from condemnation, there comes a change in the quality of the breath he draws and the substance he takes from the ethers. As he rises higher in his thinking, the lungs are refined, become sensitive to a finer texture of air, which in turn, acts upon the blood and skin. *It is the fine, high tone of thought that causes the body to throw off its waste products more easily and quickly.*

Praise and thanksgiving cleanse and free the mind and also aid in cleansing and freeing waste matter from the body. Thanksgiving and praise have a releasing, freeing effect upon the whole body temple. *The bodily functions in the abdominal region especially respond to praise.* Just as both adults and children often are emotionally starved for kindness, appreciation and praise, so are the organs of the body. A doctor once told me that praise can heal constipation, as well as other diseases of the abdominal region.

THE BENEFITS OF PROPER ELIMINATION

The power of elimination is a heavenly gift. You are constantly working to eliminate obstacles, both in your habitual thinking and in your outer world of affairs and relationships. Elimination is your power for casting off that which you have outgrown in life to overcome all obstacles and to be victorious in every endeavor as you affirm: "I AM LETTING THE CHRIST MIND DO ITS FREEING WORK IN ME NOW."

A change of mind effects a corresponding change in the body. If the thoughts are lifted up, the whole organism is raised to a higher vibration. If the system has been burdened with congestion, the highest life energy will give it freedom. But there must be a renunciation or letting go of old thoughts before the new can find a place in consciousness. This is a psychological law which has its outer expression in the intricate elimination functions of the body. Renunciation does not mean the abandonment of happy, gracious living, but rather is the giving up of deeply-rooted negative thoughts and feelings.

A healthy state of mind is attained and maintained when the thinker willingly lets go of the old thoughts and takes on new and better ones. Living old thoughts over and over keeps the inlet for new thoughts closed. Then crystallization sets in. Tuberculosis, cancer, tumors and many other ills of the flesh are evidence that nature has been outraged and is protesting and stirring to free itself from old, worn-out attitudes. The prevailing ills of the abdominal region — constipation, tumors and the like — are caused by constriction of the whole body energy.

When freedom is declared and the mind power of elimination establishes that freedom in the emotions and body of man, a sweetness and lightness is seen in the whole organism as a strength and elasticity develops.

The mind power of elimination is constantly infusing more energy into one's being and at the same time casting out of mind and body all waste. The forgiving love of the Christ spirit is not only a wonderful spiritual stimulant for soul and body, it is also an important factor in the elimination process. It causes an inrushing of the new as a letting go of the old takes place.

When the law of forgiveness is satisfied, it draws new life, strength and power from the divine source and throws off the old. Holding on to thoughts of unhappiness, sin, sickness, and poverty is the cause of much of the inharmony that exists today. When new light is born in consciousness, the old error thought loses its grasp and falls away.

You need to realize that the passing away of the old and the incoming of the new are results of the outworking of God's law of good in your life. You should assist in bringing about these changes rather than fighting them! As you practice forgiveness, you will realize that you are letting go of all weariness, doubt, fear, and you will feel a lightness and freedom in your whole being.

GAINING FREEDOM FROM THE POSSESSIVENESS THAT MAKES YOU SICK

Your mind power of elimination lets you know when there is something you should let go or eliminate. *When you have physical pain or discomfort in the organs of elimination, the mind power of renunciation is trying to warn you to let go and give up some old attitude, experience or relationship.* If you do let go, you will be shown the way to healing. If you hold on, healing will not come permanently until you let go, no matter what else you do.

Sometimes health problems in the abdominal region are caused by possessiveness. When you feel the bondage of possessiveness, it is also an indication that you are being possessive of another. Anytime you feel bound, you are also binding. You can have the complete freedom from possessiveness when you personally are willing to stop holding fast and dictating to other people.

When you feel bound by the possessiveness of other people and suddenly feel compelled to get free from it, begin to decree to those who seem to be dominating you: "I FULLY AND FREELY RELEASE YOU. I LOOSE YOU AND LET YOU GO. I LET GO AND LET GOD BRING FREEDOM INTO THIS RELATIONSHIP NOW."

But do not stop there! Affirm for the one who seems to be possessing you: "YOU FULLY AND FREELY RELEASE ME. YOU LOOSE ME AND LET ME GO. YOU LET GO AND LET GOD BRING FREEDOM INTO THIS RELATIONSHIP NOW."

In this simple way you can begin to get and give emotional freedom which leads to healing in mind and body as well.

GIVE EMOTIONAL FREEDOM TO OTHERS
AND BENEFIT YOURSELF

Bondage and inharmony come in your human relationships when you try to reform, hang on to, mold others to your wishes. *It is time for you to stop worrying about others and go inside yourself to do the changing!*

The first step, after going inside yourself to make changes, is to loose your loved ones and let them go to their good. At first this may seem the very thing you do not want to do. You feel that they need your encouragement, help and understanding. But, when you attempt to help them by keeping a possessive hold on them, they chafe so under your restraint that they are not free to love you as they would otherwise do.

Love that binds another against his will can never result in happiness for either person; whereas a love that releases its own to their highest good brings ever closer those souls who are one in spirit.

When a wife thinks of her husband, she should not condemn him nor think of him as hers alone, but as a child of God. Then, she should pour out upon him the highest, most unselfish love possible. In this way she frees him and herself, so they may truly be one in God's love.

Sometimes a mother hangs on to her children to such an extent as to hinder their development and her own. As they grow up she frantically tries to hold their love and interest by appealing to their sense of obligation. It is not by such demands that one experiences real love.

The self that Jesus of Nazareth taught must be denied is the *grasping personality.* It must let go its hold upon possessive attitudes before there can be harmonious activity in the elimination center; it must let go its possessive hold upon people before one's problems can be resolved.

FREEDOM BRINGS HEALING OF ALCOHOLISM

I once watched this principle work in a husband-wife relationship. The wife had become very possessive, suspicious and jealous of her husband; she had bound him with her negative feelings. Being a sensitive soul, he began to feel that bondage. Always when we feel bound, we fight back, trying to gain freedom. Her husband fought back by beginning to drink heavily.

This wife did everything in her power to convince her husband to stop drinking, but he only grew worse. Finally through the help of a spiritual counselor, she learned she must free her husband emotionally and trust him mentally; that when he felt that freedom he would stop drinking.

For this purpose she began daily declaring: "I CAST THIS BURDEN ON THE CHRIST IN YOU, AND I GO FREE AND YOU GO FREE." She also stopped reacting negatively to his drinking bouts, no longer talked to him about them, nor questioned his comings and goings. Instead she told him plainly he was free to do as he pleased. As she mentally unbound him, his drinking immediately diminished and soon ceased altogether.

You never lose anything that still belongs to you by divine right through the act of release. Instead, you make way for your good to manifest in grander ways than ever before!

Indeed, the function of the mind power of elimination is twofold—to eliminate error and then to expand your good. Elimination of something from your life is always an indication that something better is on the way! When there is elimination in your life, it is an indication that your good is trying to expand. Knowing this makes it easier to let go the old and let your new good appear. At such times declare "I LET GO AND TRUST."

HOW TO CLEANSE AND PURIFY
YOURSELF FOR A HEALING

When you are trying to achieve a result, realize a heart's desire, or regain your health and it has not come, it is often because there is still something in mind, body, affairs or relationships that you need to renounce, free, release, or eliminate. When you do, you will get results. As long as you put off this elimination process, you put off results, no matter what else you do!

Every phase of life involves renunciation. Every advance means the rejection of something old, especially when that "advance" is to be a healing! In the body, unless elimination is maintained, there will be no new growth, no new cells, no healthy flow of life forces. *There is a constant need in your life for elimination which cleanses and makes way for expansion of good.*

As someone wailed, "It is so painful, this letting go." True! It can be a crucifying experience to let go of that which is familiar, even though you have outgrown it. Thaddeus was the disciple of Jesus who symbolized the mind power of elimination and his name means "praising, confessing, courageous." Letting go takes courage.

However, the mind power of renunciation not only eliminates the old, but it also expands the new. It will not leave you desolate, if you do your part. It not only takes something from you, but gives something to you!

Furthermore, when you do not willingly let go in your life of that which is no longer for your highest good, then that which you have outgrown leaves you anyway. If you clutch or try to possess people, they find a way to get away; hospitals, mental institutions and cemeteries are filled with people who wanted freedom from possessiveness and got it.

Elimination is the power in the mind of man to cleanse and free him. For this purpose, relax often, direct your attention to the abdominal region and declare: "I AM BLESSED WITH PERFECT ELIMINATION IN MIND, BODY AND AFFAIRS NOW."

Your healing power of

ETERNAL LIFE

— 13 —

Two ladies were chatting. One said, "What is the first thing you would do if you had just been told by your doctor that you only had six months to live?"

"That's simple," was the reply. "I would get another doctor!"

It is sometimes a surprise to people to learn that life itself is a mind power whose center of activity in the body is located in the generative organs.

We have usually considered life as a mysterious quality, which some people have in abundance and which others possess only meagerly. Although the dictionary doesn't seem sure just what this thing called life is, it generally describes life as "that vital force, whether regarded as physical or spiritual." Life is the state of being alive, which one's state of mind surely influences.

It is quite logical that the mind power of life would be located in the generative organs of the body as shown in Figure 13-1. It is these organs that are responsible for

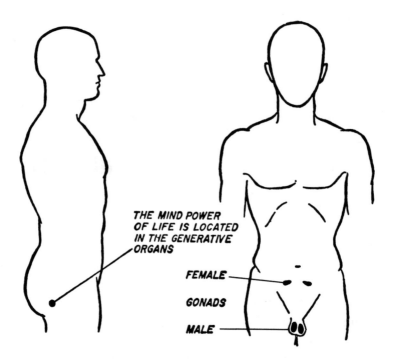

THE MIND POWER
OF LIFE IS LOCATED
IN THE GENERATIVE
ORGANS

FEMALE

GONADS

MALE

Figure 13–1.   Location of the Mind Powers of LIFE.

bringing forth new life to this earth and for affecting the
health and vitality of those souls once they arrive. Thus,
right use of the mind power of life in man is very important if he is to enjoy health and vitality.

When Jesus of Nazareth said, "I AM THE RESURRECTION
AND THE LIFE," He may have been using a mental technique, that of telling the power of His mind to awaken His
whole body to new life. (John 11:25) This resurrection
process is available to all of us. *If you ever doubt that life
is a mind power, just take the word "life" and declare it*

over and over. You will feel a new surge of enthusiastic life well up within you.

The best method of activating the mighty life force within you is this: in your quiet times of relaxation and rest, start at the top of the head and mentally go down through the various parts of the body, decreeing "LIFE, LIFE, LIFE." As you decree it, you will feel a certain current of excitement, enthusiasm, and a warm electrical energy come alive within you in various parts of the body.

Charles Fillmore explained how he did this when nearing the age of 50:

> "The belief in old age began to take hold of me when I was nearing the half-century mark. I began to get wrinkled and gray, my knees tottered, and a great weakness came over me . . . I spent hours and hours silently affirming my unity with the infinite energy of the one true God. I associated with the young . . . In this way I switched the old age current of thought. Then I went deep down within my body and talked to the inner life centers. I told them with firmness and decision that I would never submit to the old age devil, that I was determined never to give in. Gradually, I felt a new life current coming up from the life center. It was a faint little stream growing strong by leaps and bounds. My cheeks have filled out, the wrinkles and crow's feet are gone, and I actually feel like the boy that I am."[1]

Men of science are now saying that life is a mind power, that it is a mental quality within you. Realizing this, you can begin to tap that life force and release it into the organs and cells of your body. Scientists now

---

1. James Dillet Freeman, *The Story of Unity* (Unity Village, MO: Unity Books, 1951, revised 1978), p.199.

state that there are vast, untapped energies sealed up in the body.

Way back in the 1890's, as related in Chapter 1, Myrtle Fillmore proved this as she released these untapped energies through the spoken word. By talking to her body, telling it that it could become perfect again, she healed herself of an incurable condition.

When you feel tired, run down, discouraged, that is the time to call upon the mind power of life within you. This power to resurrect new energy is not a supernatural one. In each cell and atom of your body is life, substance and intelligence. As you speak words of "life," each cell responds. You can charge the cells of your body with life because they are receptive and always listening. If you dwell upon the idea of life, your body takes up this idea and acts upon it, first consciously and then subconsciously. The idea of life will then work through the cells of your body, generating new energy.

A DYING WOMAN BROUGHT BACK FROM THE EDGE OF DEATH

A woman was dying from bronchial pneumonia, attended by a violent fever, pains and chills. Then congestion in her lungs set in, affecting her breathing and heart action. In spite of the finest medical care, this lady was slipping away and a relative asked a spiritual counselor to begin praying for her. Over and over the counselor affirmed, "LIFE! LIFE! LIFE! YOU CANNOT DIE. YOU LIVE AND FULFILL THE DIVINE PLAN OF YOUR LIFE. NOTHING CAN TAKE LIFE FROM YOU."

Later, when again praying for the ill woman, the counselor had the impression of being in strange surroundings in an atmosphere quite unlike that of this world. The sick woman was the only person she could see off in the distance. The counselor became alarmed as she realized that though blissfully happy, this sick woman was getting further and further away and within a few moments, might be beyond recall.

First, the counselor tried to talk to the ill woman, but could not get her attention as she continued moving further away. Finally the counselor decreed loudly: "YOU CANNOT LEAVE LIFE. COME BACK AND FINISH YOUR WORK! FULFILL YOUR DIVINE PLAN." She then felt a jerking sensation, as though the sick woman had suddenly been brought back onto this earth plane.

The dying woman later related this experience:

"My throat began to fill up again and, not having sufficient strength to cough, I lost my breath and seemed to be smothering. In an instant, I saw my spirit leave my body. In such a blissful state, I had no desire to return to my body of flesh. Then I heard a voice say, 'Live! Come back to your body of flesh, and fulfill your divine plan.' Instantly I was back in my body of flesh, but entered very reluctantly, for in entering through the top of the head in the same way that the spirit had left, my body shook from head to foot and for several days I did not seem to be firmly established in my body."

She did not die—she fully recovered.

ACTIVATE YOUR ATOMIC ENERGY

Through the power of your thoughts and words, you can penetrate and release unlimited energy that is pent up in the atoms of your body, and you will be astounded at the response. Lifeless functions anywhere in the body can be restored to action by one's speaking to the intelligence and life within them.

One scientist, who has spent much time studying the atomic structure of the body, has said that your body is made up of trillions of atoms. At the center of each atom in your body there is a central light around which lesser lights are constantly circling. At the center of each one of these atoms is life and energy. When you affirm "LIFE" you stir up and bring into action that tremendous atomic energy in your body. Indeed, when you affirm the word "LIFE," you are working with an atomic energy that is all powerful, because you are an atomic being!

Most of our ill health, both physical and mental, is caused by our lack of understanding of the true nature of life. Man is only partially alive because he does not understand that he can call forth the life force within him. When you turn your thinking toward the idea of life, you shall experience a different feeling and a different quality of life. You can start a rejuvenation in your body and in your world.

These powerful affirmations have helped people all over the world to release the rejuvenating power of life within them:

"LIFE! LIFE! LIFE! I AM FILLED AND THRILLED WITH VITALIZING LIFE!"

"I AM ALIVE, ALERT, AWAKE, JOYOUS, AND ENTHUSIASTIC ABOUT LIFE."

"I AM THE EVER-RENEWING, THE EVER-UNFOLDING EXPRESSION OF INFINITE LIFE."

To think intently upon "life" is to quicken it into action. To talk about energy, force, and power will cause the life currents to flow swiftly throughout the whole being. So forget about growing old and begin to really live!

In her book, *Dare to Believe*,[2] May Rowland relates the story of a woman who was informed by her doctor:

"That pain in your leg is caused by old age."

"Nonsense," she replied. "My other leg is the same age, and it doesn't hurt a bit!"

REJUVENATE EVERY PHASE OF YOUR LIFE

Do not let inactive ideas clog your mind, but open your thinking to the idea of life and let new, creative, life-giving ideas express in and through you. Decree often: "MY MIND, BODY AND AFFAIRS ARE NOW FILLED WITH REJUVENATING LIFE. I AM FILLED AND THRILLED WITH RE-JUVENATING LIFE!" You can actually transform your mind, body and affairs, bringing alive an electrical energy and activity of tremendous good within them through the use of this affirmation.

Affirming life can especially rejuvenate your affairs of all types, as well as your health. Our attraction to life is so strong that we instinctively shrink from listless people who are lacking in vitality and enthusiasm for life. They bore us. However, we are irresistibly drawn to lively people. And, rightly so. The word "life" denotes activity, movement, excitement. If you ever feel bored with your world, affirm "life" and things will begin to happen. You will be drawn into the stream of life; you will find yourself "where the action is."

2. May Rowland, *Dare to Believe* (Unity Village, MO.: Unity School of Christianity).

A CASE OF SYPHILIS HEALED

When there is disease in the organs of life in the body, those difficulties can often be overcome as you affirm life for yourself, or even for others.

A man visited a spiritual counselor, asking if anything could be done to relieve him of a disease which his doctors had declared as incurable — predating the era of the miracles of modern medicine.

The counselor assured him that nothing was impossible with God. In great pain in his back, this man was suffering intensely. Part of his lips had been eaten away by the disease and the lobe of one ear, and other areas of the body has also been attacked.

The counselor became quiet and prayed with this man for guidance. In prayer she decreed that the cleansing power of the Spirit within him was now working in and through every cell of his body; that all impurity was being cleared away. As she was meditating, suddenly the word "syphilis" flashed to her.

Realizing that this man had been attacked by this disease in the organs of life, she suggested that he go home and spend three days in prayer, affirming life and believing he could be healed. She told him to intently study the healings of Jesus as given in the Four Gospels, to meditate upon those healings which most appealed to him, and for at least four hours out of every 24 affirm over and over:

"I NOW CONSECRATE MY MIND AND BODY TO YOU, DEAR FATHER. I AM NOW WILLING AND READY TO GIVE UP THE OLD WAYS, THE FALSE BELIEFS THAT HAVE BOUND ME. I AM NOW READY TO TAKE THE NEW HIGHER LIFE FROM UNIVERSAL MIND. DEAR FATHER, I KNOW YOU HAVE FORGIVEN ALL MY MISTAKES AND ARE SEEING IN ME ONLY MY PERFECT SELF

WHICH IS PURE. I NOW SEE ONLY MY PURE, PERFECT SELF,
AS IT SHINES ITS RADIANT LIGHT INTO EVERY CELL OF MY
BODY. I AM CLEAN AND PURE, HEALTHY AND FREE. YES,
PRAISE GOD, I AM FREE!"

This man faithfully followed this spiritual prescription
and when he returned the third day, the lobe of his ear,
lips, and other parts of his body were free from inflammation. As he continued to dwell upon the spiritual side
of life, both within and around him, he became an entirely changed man. Gradually his Higher Nature of
Eternal Life came into physical expression as he over-
came the incurable diagnosis, and regained his health
completely.

THE "CHANGE OF LIFE"—HOW TO DEAL WITH IT

What people call the "change of life" is an experience
that can be met much more easily when one affirms
"life."

Some things concerning the physical expression of life
should always be held sacred. The change of life is one
of them. As easily as one season blends into another, so
does one period of life merge into another. The change
of life, which affects both man and woman, is in reality
a time of soul growth and freedom into expanded good.

Following the physical and psychological changes that
take place at this period in life, many a person has risen
to new heights. For many, life truly begins at this period.
One should welcome this change! Affirm: "ALL CHANGE
IN MY LIFE IS PERFECTLY TIMED. ALL CHANGE IN MY LIFE
IS IN ACCORD WITH GOD'S EVER-INCREASING GOOD FOR ME.
I GO THROUGH ALL CHANGES EASILY TO MEET MY SUPREME
GOOD."

The following is suggested for the change of life experience: "FATHER, I THANK THEE FOR THE ORDERLY ADJUSTMENT OF EVERY FUNCTION OF MY BODY. I THANK THEE FOR THE NEW LIFE THAT I AM ENTERING. I WILLINGLY LET GO OF THE OLD AND GLADLY LAY HOLD OF THE NEW. LET THY PERFECT WILL BE DONE IN ME NOW."

A housewife had great difficulty in her monthly periods; she also suffered headaches, as though she had a band around her head. A search into her personal relationships revealed that her husband jealously resented and depreciated her talents. When she realized this, she began declaring for her husband: "YOU AND I ARE ONE, AND ALL PRAISE GIVEN TO ME IS ALSO FOR YOU." Freedom soon came from further discomfort in both the generative organs and head.

CAUSE OF FEMALE TROUBLE AND STERILITY

One of the great mental and emotional causes of illness in the organs of generation in the body is a feeling of limitation and bondage. What we commonly hear described as "female trouble" is often the result of feeling restricted. That person is probably being dominated by another member of her family or is trying to dominate another. The mind power of life in the generative functions feels that bondage and reacts as lack-of-ease in the body.

Disease in the female organs can be caused by a hidden resentment toward a husband, son, father or another member of the opposite sex. *When the mind of a woman is not gentle and soft, but hard and cold in her attitudes, the fertility rate is low. Resentment from members of the opposite sex can also cause female health problems.*

Recent clinical tests suggest that emotional conflicts —hatred, fear, anxiety, poor adjustment to marriage —all can cause sterility. These emotional states, it is believed, may have prevented conception in from one-quarter to one-third of all cases of involuntary childlessness. Once they are removed, pregnancy becomes possible.

It is through the function of the fallopian tubes that union of the male and female cells must take place, if a child is to be conceived. In high-strung women, the tubes are sometimes tightly shut, apparently because of nervous tension. When the tubes are closed, no meeting of male and female cells is possible. Even if the tubes remain open and a union of the cells takes place, in exceptionally nervous tense women the lining of the uterus, which should be soft and relaxed, may be so taut that it offers no anchorage on which the potential baby can start growth. In such cases, pregnancy will not take place.

Psychiatrists feel that in many families where psychic sterility is found there are often strong parental prohibitions against sex that cause the children to continue to be inhibited in concepts of sex as well as in their marital relationships.

There once was a sensitive woman who remained childless in her first marriage, but in a later marriage she had several children. The psychiatric explanation was that conscious or hidden hostility toward the first husband led to a closing of the fallopian tubes. The second, happier marriage brought about mental and physical relaxation and made conception possible.

A "sterile" wife who consciously wanted to have children, hated her mother-in-law who had often let her know of a desire to become a grandmother. This bitter woman's sterility seemed to be her way subconsciously of withholding from her mother-in-law that which she desired most.

Impotence and other health problems in men can often be traced to hostility toward the opposite sex which may stem from childhood. Since the mind power of will located in the front forehead is closely connected with the mind power of life located in the generative organs, a willful hostility can reflect its unhappy pattern in the sex organs in many ways.

THE HEALING OF A DISEASED PROSTATE

In his book *You Can Heal Yourself,*[3] the famous Japanese metaphysician Dr. Masaharu Taniguchi relates the case of a man with prostate cancer, the location of which made an operation impossible.

While in great pain, this suffering man learned of a lecture on healing to be delivered in his neighborhood and in desperation attended. But as the lecture was being delivered, he found himself in such pain that he clung to the person nearest him. When he explained why, that person rushed up to the lecturer and said, "There is a man in the audience suffering from prostate cancer. What should he do to be healed?"

"Disease of the sexual area, such as prostate gland cancer, often represents a 'triangle' relationship," was the lecturer's reply.

"Will he be cured if he confesses?" was the next question.

"Yes, sins disappear when they are confessed. Error does not really exist. Therefore, it disappears." This was the metaphysical answer.

---

3. Taniguchi, (Tokyo, Japan: Seicho-no Ie Foundation, 1961).

The sick man then confessed before all assembled that there *was* a triangular relationship; that he had had an affair with his wife's maid and had decided he wanted to marry her. He had even hired another man to try to lure his wife into adultery, hoping to gain evidence for a divorce. But his wife not only resisted the other man's attentions, but had innocently reported them to her husband!

Finally the wife learned of her husband's affair and discharged the maid. Thereafter, a long period of emotional strife and much quarreling existed between them, during which time the husband developed prostate gland cancer.

The audience was moved by this man's confession and prayed for him. All pain left following the confession and prayers. He returned home to sleep soundly and painlessly for the first time in weeks. The next morning he asked his wife's forgiveness, and she asked his. Later, when the pain did not return, he realized he had been healed and commented, "It was certainly a miracle that someone like myself, with so little knowledge of the Truth, should have been cured so completely."

A REPORTED HEALING OF UTERINE CANCER

Still another instance that Dr. Taniguchi relates is that of a young Japanese housewife who was informed she had cancer of the uterus, and it was so far advanced that medical treatment could not help her very much. A sister, who was a healing Truth student, explained that another type of emotional triangle was the cause. This young wife resented her mother-in-law and had not allowed her to live with them. According to an old Oriental tradition, she should do so.

The sick woman finally realized her selfishness and asked her mother-in-law to return, insisting all previous inharmony had been her fault. Of course, the mother-in-law was overjoyed and a high state of happiness was established in this family group.

Shortly thereafter, this young wife, who was still confined to bed, discharged a large flow of substance or secretion resulting from the diseased uterine condition. This proved to be a part of the cure. From that point on, she regained her health steadily and later her doctor stated that the recovery should be considered a divine miracle.

Deep emotional conflicts produce what is considered incurable diseases in the generative organs of the body. When that "incurable" conflict is cleared up, so is the attending or corresponding disease!

CHILDREN HAVE PRENATAL MEMORY

An attitude toward or concerning conception of a child can cause listlessness in that child years later, as well as emotional problems. Prenatal studies now claim that the souls of unborn children have consciousness from the time of conception and they subconsciously know their parents' attitudes toward them from conception on! Years later those children often reflect the prenatal hostility they had subconsciously absorbed while in the womb, producing both health and behavior problems.

A young child was failing in school. His parents sought help from a spiritual counselor who asked, "Did you rejoice when you learned you had conceived a child?"

Taken by surprise, the parents confessed they had not.

The child had been conceived during the immediate post-war years when everything was in a turmoil. They had even considered abortion. It was into this unwanted atmosphere that the child had been born.

The counselor advised, "Apologize to your child—both silently to his subconscious memory in which is stored the feeling of being unwanted at birth, and also consciously love and appreciate him. He came into the world selecting you as his parents for a divine reason. He is a gift from God. Let him know it!"

Mentally the mother said to her listless little boy: "Forgive me, dear. Mother wanted to kill you. Yet you selected me as being the most suitable person in the world to be your mother. In spite of this I continued to think I did not want you, but I did. Please forgive me and I will become a wonderful mother to you. I promise." Consciously both parents began to speak words of love, praise, and appreciation to their young son.

This child was soon eagerly doing his homework without any persuasion from his parents. His marks improved tremendously as the parents continued to praise him, assuring him of their love.

PSYCHIC OBSESSIONS HAVE A SEXUAL BASIS

Sex energy is actually soul energy seeking expression through the higher nature of man.[4] When it is restricted or dammed up in some way it then expresses anyway, but as complexes, fixations, neurotic attachments, warping the personality, emotional nature and health of a person.

---

4. See the chapter on Sex in *The Prosperity Secrets of the Ages.*

As noted psychic psychoanalyst, Nandor Fodor, pointed out in his book, *The Haunted Mind,*[5] psychic obsessions occur in people who are sexually frustrated— usually women. Of the psychic obsessions which I have encountered over the years, each case was that of a confused woman who was sexually frustrated. Two cases were those of women who considered themselves "too spiritual" to remain married. At least, that had become their excuse for their deep-seated hostility toward sex, which probably had a chidhood basis and for which they needed psychiatric treatment. In both instances, these women had gotten involved with a third woman who claimed she was "too spiritual" to stay married; she had divorced her husband. (Such misguided souls have been described as "sexless saints sitting in judgment on passionate sins.") Although this third woman considered herself "too spiritual" to remain married to a fine husband, she did not consider herself "too spiritual" to take on another "highly spiritual" woman as her "lover."

Freud, Jung and Adler all agreed that along with the false mental fixations that have settled in the subconscious area of the mind, the conscious mind also has a number of false mental fixations. When those conscious and subconscious fixations which have a sexual basis come to the surface, psychic obsessions which are a form of retreat from reality, occur. The one experiencing them claims these obsessions result from their supposed high-powered spirituality, when in reality they are only a result of their sexual frustrations.

The ancient priests termed these obsessions as "having a demon" and through a special ritual of exorcism were often able to cast them out, as did Jesus. In modern

5. Nandor Fodor, *The Haunted Mind,* (New York: Garrett Publications).

times, psychiatric treatment has usually been the most successful solution. Metaphysically, a fine healing treatment for the obsessed consists of affirming for them: "THE PEACE OF THE CHRIST SPIRIT IS POURED OUT UPON YOU. YOU ARE AT PEACE IN YOUR MIND AND IN YOUR BODY."

HOW TO UPLIFT YOUR LIFE FORCE

People who relate or listen to "dirty jokes" are opening their minds and bodies to health problems in the sex organs. *Impurity of mind works itself out as impurity of body.* A housewife who was sterile and remained childless, later had to have a breast removed. She delighted in off-color stories and unknowingly proved that impurity of mind manifests as impurity of body in the sex organs.

One's ears should be closed to all suggestions of unclean talk, scandal and gossip concerning the sensual actions of others, if one wishes to remain free of disease in the sex organs.

Judas is the disciple symbolizing the force located in the generative organs. When we have betrayed that life force through misuse—either as physical or emotional dissipation by dwelling upon the sensual and negative—there is still hope for redeeming and uplifting the life force.

The will, located in the front forehead, and the zeal center, located in the back of the neck, are both closely connected with the life center in the generative organs and can help uplift that creative energy, *pulling it up through the whole body into the superconsicous mind at the crown of the head.* As creative energy is drawn upward into the subconscious functions of the solar plexus region, into the conscious functions of the mind in the front forehead and five senses, and finally in the super-conscious functions of the crown of the head, this creative energy is directed constructively. The spinal cord is a cable to conduct energy. Through it, the seminal fluids flow through the nervous system, connecting mind and body.

As you dwell upon the word "life," the life force in the generative functions is uplifted and distributed to all parts of the soul and body as a vitalizing force. It ascends the spinal cord, flowing out over the thousand nerve tributaries leading from the spinal cord to every organ of the body.

TO THINK UPON "LIFE"
QUICKENS IT INTO ACTION

To affirm "life" will make the life force flow swiftly throughout the whole being: "LIFE CHARGES MY MIND, FLOWS THROUGH MY VEINS, PERMEATES MY TISSUES, NERVES, MUSCLES, CELLS. MY EYES SHINE, MY SKIN GLOWS, MY WHOLE BODY RADIATES HEALTH."

All other glands seem closely related to the gonads, consisting of the male testes and the female ovaries. Apparently the personality and temperament of an individual, as well as the state of his other glands, depend upon the state of the mind power of life located in the sex organs.

In each cell and atom of the body there is life, substance and intelligence. You speak a word of life, and each cell responds. You can charge the cells of the body with life. If you present the idea of life, your body takes up this idea and acts upon it.

The reactions of uterus and ovaries in the sexual

organs and the reaction of the mammary glands in the chest to the pituitary gland at the base of the brain show a close relationship. Thus, the organs of generation should be carefully guarded against misuse. Generative organs are centers of purity. When their substance is wasted, they become the vortex of destructive problems of both mind and body. The words "sacred" and "secret" have the same root. One's sex life should be held sacred, thus secret.

There is an ancient teaching among the Chinese mystics that the life force in man, when conserved, becomes transmuted into a finer soul and body essence. Increased health and spiritual understanding result. The foregoing mental treatments on "life" help you to accomplish that.

Conclusion:

THE RESULTS OF DEVELOPING YOUR MIND POWERS

Let the end of this book be only the beginning — of one of the most fascinating experiences of your life.

Now that you know *what* your mind powers are, *where* they are located, and *how* you can develop them, get busy!

Once when I was passing through the deep waters of severe personal loss, the study of these 12 mind powers fortified me with added strength which gave way to hope for happier days ahead. That hope has been fulfilled.

So do not underestimate your fascinating mind powers. As you study and unfold them, they can lift you out of hopeless despair into a "brave new world" of increased health, abundance, and far more happiness than you have previously dreamed possible!

A friend of mine has had tremendous success in personally helping countless people overcome their problems through prayer. His success formula is simple. He begins by having the troubled person relax; together they activate the 12 mind powers within that person through affirmation. Later, when they pray together about the specific problem, it is often resolved quickly. His explanation is that by arousing the 12 mind powers first, the troubled person automatically releases a super-intelligence to work for and through him not ordinarily tapped, and he is then able to meet life victoriously.

And so I say again, "Get busy" and then "Get ready" for one of the most rewarding experiences of your life!

HOW TO "RELAX AND LET GO"

Go at it the easy way. In developing your mind powers "easy does it."

Either on a slant board or reclining in the comfort of your bed, first quietly tell your mind and body to "RELAX AND LET GO." It is good to speak to the mind and body as though you were speaking to a friend whom you wished to help. You might say: "RELAX AND LET GO ALL TENSION, STRESS AND STRAIN. RELAX AND LET GO ALL INHARMONIES OF MIND AND BODY. RELAX AND LET GO."

Then, breathing deeply, sink down mentally and emotionally into that restful state as you direct your attention from the top of the head, down through the body, into the tips of the toes, gently declaring, "YOU RELAX AND LET GO." If worries try to get your attention, dismiss them gently saying to them, "RELAX AND LET GO."

You can next release a super-intelligence into your mind and body from the Christ Mind at the top of the head by reminding yourself, "I AM DIVINE INTELLIGENCE. I AM LETTING DIVINE INTELLIGENCE EXPRESS PERFECTLY

THROUGH ME NOW." Or you might prefer these affirmations: "I AM THE CHRIST MIND, I AM! I AM! I AM! I AM LETTING THE CHRIST MIND EXPRESS PERFECTLY THROUGH ME NOW."

Sweep your whole body with this idea from head to foot. This act brings alive the super-wisdom within all areas of your body. It arouses your mind powers, so that they quickly get ready to respond to your "call."

When you have gotten your mind and body quiet, peaceful and alert, you are then ready to call alive any of the mind powers which you particularly wish to activate. (Though through your general study of mental and spiritual subjects, they may have already had preliminary activity.) Remember that your 12 mind power are like people: they can be praised and blessed into much work for you, but they rebel against force. When you gently and lovingly begin to give them your attention and recognition, they will respond but in their own time and way. They will not be forced, rushed or dictated to.

HOW TO ACTIVATE YOUR 12 SUPER-MIND POWERS FOR HEALING

Gently activate them after relaxing, "calling" them lovingly, without pressure. It is usually a good practice to begin by gently calling each of the 12 mind powers briefly. Simply call the name of the mind power and let your attention dwell upon that area of the body:

Begin with "FAITH" in the pineal gland at the center of the head; then "STRENGTH" at the small of the back; "JUSTICE" at the pit of the stomach; "LOVE" at the heart; "POWER" at the root of the tongue; "IMAGINATION" between the eyes; "WILL" and "UNDERSTANDING" in the front forehead; "ORDER" back of the navel; "ZEAL" at the base of the brain; "ELIMINATION" at the base of the spinal column; and last, "LIFE" in the generative functions of the lower abdomen.

Next, if there are health problems in some special area, call on the mind power in that area. For instance, call over and over the word "LOVE, LOVE, LOVE" as you gently direct your attention to the heart. This daily practice can begin to alleviate heart trouble and its emotional causes, as it releases tension, stress and strain in that area, replacing it with the activated mind power of love.

By calling over and over the word "POWER, POWER, POWER," you will find increased mental, spiritual and physical power being activated and released through the throat area into the entire body. You will discover that you have increased physical and mental energy by "calling" this mind power into activity.

I was reminded of this while writing the chapter on "Power." During the days that I worked on that subject, I discovered I had so much increased energy that I constantly cleaned my apartment in an effort to release that increased energy, though a competent housekeeper had done my housecleaning for years!

If you have a need for more physical and emotional strength, you can bring it alive as you give your attention to the word "STRENGTH, STRENGTH, STRENGTH," while focusing your attention at the small of the back.

At the time I wrote the chapter dealing with "Strength," I was praying for the mental and physical strength to complete the entire book, while facing increased mental and emotional demands upon my time and energy. One day while lying on my slant board affirming, "STRENGTH, STRENGTH, STRENGTH," I noticed that the strength center at the small of the back had begun to vibrate, releasing what seemed an electric energy into my mind and body. Thereafter, while completing this manuscript chapter by chapter, at moments when either emotional or physical vitality seemed low, I found that I was quickly recharged by relaxing and again dwelling upon the thought, "STRENGTH, STRENGTH, STRENGTH." Each time, that electrical energy again flowed into mind and body from the strength mind power at the small of the back.

After completing the general "calling" of your 12 mind powers,[1] and then dwelling upon any particular one or ones that are related to certain health problems, it is good to conclude by relaxing completely and sweeping your whole being with the thought of "JOY." This helps the activated mind powers within to be freed to work for you in the conscious, subconscious and superconscious levels of the mind. After declaring, "THE JOY OF THE LORD IS A WELLSPRING WITHIN ME, NOW ESTABLISHING PERFECT RESULTS," and mentally pouring forth this idea of "JOY" from head to foot, it is time to arise and become actively engaged in outer work again.

HOW TO TIME YOUR HEALING MEDITATIONS

When you first begin developing your mind powers in daily affirmation, do so for only a short time; then gradually lengthen your time of relaxation and affirmation, remembering to remain relaxed throughout the

---

1. The meditation cassette by May Rowland, *Come Ye Apart Awhile*, available from Unity School of Christianity, Unity Village, Missouri, is especially helpful for familiarizing you with your 12 mind powers and calling them forth in prayer and meditation.

process. If you become tense or "heady" while calling your mind powers, it is usually wise to give up the practice for the time being and go back to your daily activities. You will usually get an inner leading on just how long to dwell daily upon this practice.

One thing you will notice in the process: That the mind powers located in the abdominal-subconscious region of the body will respond much more quickly to your "call" of them—strength at the small of the back, judgment at the pit of the stomach, love in the chest-lungs-heart area, etc.—than the more interior mind powers located in the area of the conscious mind in the intellectual area of the head. The reason, of course, is obvious. The emotions are always quicker to respond than the intellect of man. Thus, the emotional mind powers located in the chest and abdomen would be quicker to respond than the intellectual mind powers in the cranium.

You will also discover that though there will gradually be a general awakening of the life forces throughout the body as you daily call on your mind powers, the more pronounced awakening will first take place at the great solar plexus region, in the seat of the subconscious, back of the heart and stomach. The solar plexus is the great "body brain" and substance center in the body and as it is mentally aroused, it imparts fresh energy and intelligence to the entire body.

When this vibratory activity becomes known to you, though it seems a strange, almost uncomfortable, sensation, you can rejoice knowing your mind powers have begun to work for and through you! Later there will doubtless be various vibratory activities occurring in other parts of the body—a further indication of your awakened mind powers.

THE VAST BENEFITS OF DEVELOPING
YOUR MIND POWERS

Believe me, these dynamic mind powers are not mere theory. They exist! They only ask to be given your attention in order to become your faithful servants, quietly supplying your mind and body with renewed inspiration and vitality. As you quietly develop them, day in and day out, month in and month out, your health will improve as will every phase of your life. These powers will gladly give you a quick lift, a fast pickup. Furthermore, you will find yourself able to relax more quickly in both mind and body. A deeper sensitivity and awareness will permeate both your mind and body; a new strength, a deeper wisdom and a keener love of life and people will envelop your consciousness. Finally, a greater joy for living will quietly unfold within you.

In the process you will have discovered the true secret of peace of mind and health of body. As you practice turning within more and more, calling on your mind powers to come alive within you and to help you in every phase of your life, they will become such aids to you that you need never again feel alone or without hope.

People will probably unconsciously tune in to your dynamic radiations and say you have "that certain something" that makes you more vital, fascinating, and successful. Indeed, life will take on new meaning.

Please note this, however. As you first begin to develop your mind powers, you may simply feel better generally; more peaceful, powerful, strengthened, more hopeful. But as you continue developing them, your whole life will gradually respond with vast improvement.

HEALING HANDS

The fact that mind power has a tremendous effect upon the body has been brought to my attention in an interesting way since I have been writing this book on healing and the previous one. During both writings, I noticed that the very act of dwelling upon the laws and mind powers of healing seemed to call alive potent healing vibrations in my hands, which literally flowed into the pages of the manuscripts. The reports of spiritual healings which have occurred in the lives of readers who studied *The Dynamic Laws of Healing* indicate that a tremendous healing vibration *was* released into the pages of that book!

(I personally do not practice the "laying on of hands" method of spiritual healing, fine though it is. Instead, I prefer to "lay on healing ideas" through the written word, thereby reaching great numbers of people who are then shown how to help themselves through the instructions given.)

Recently a fellow minister commented, "There is something different about your hands. What is it?" When I related how a healing vibration had been activated in them while writing on the subject, she commented, "Why, of course, that is just further proof that the power of thought can arouse healing forces in the body."

Almost two decades later, when I revised this book, that same healing vibration came alive in my hands again — another further proof of the life force that is latent in the body, and which can be mentally activated.

YOU CAN TURN ON THIS SAME POWER

You have this same healing force within you to "call" alive your mind powers. Just by dwelling upon the subject of healing you, too, will begin stirring it up within you.

Now that you know the healing secret of the ages, turn to it often, and let your dynamic mind powers begin working for you and through you.

As you do, I trust that the end of this book will be only the beginning of a healthy, happy life for a new YOU!

CATHERINE PONDER
P.O. Drawer 1278
Palm Desert, CA., 92261, U.S.A.

A SPECIAL NOTE FROM THE AUTHOR

Through the generous outpouring of their tithes over the years, the readers of my books have helped me to financially establish three new churches—the most recent being a global ministry, the nondenominational *Unity Worldwide,* with headquarters in Palm Desert, California. Many thanks for your help in the past, and for all that you continue to share.

You are also invited to share your tithes with the churches of your choice—especially those which teach the truths stressed in this book. Such churches would include the metaphysical churches of Unity, Religious Science, Divine Science, Science of Mind, and other related churches, many of which are members of The International New Thought Movement. (For a list of such churches write The International New Thought Alliance, 7314 E. Stetson Drive, Scottsdale, Arizona 85251.) Your support of such churches can help spread the healing Truth that mankind is now seeking in this New Age of metaphysical enlightenment.